PRAISE FOR
PROTECT YOUR LIGHT

"George's book is one of a kind and something every lightworker needs to read! His tools and processes are truly life-changing when it comes to energy protection and enhancing your powerful light. George makes energy protection both accessible and easy to digest for the reader. Get ready for this book to up your spiritual game and help you lead a more harmonious and authentic life!"

—EMMA MUMFORD, bestselling author of *Positively Wealthy*

"*Protect Your Light* has been birthed at exactly the right time in our human evolution. George breaks everything down—in such a simple, yet profound, manner—on how to maneuver these trying times with the protection and love that is available to each and every one of us. This book will shift you and align you with your highest self so that you are free to be the lightworker your soul came to be. Mark my words, this will be your go-to guide for years to come."

—DANIELLE PAIGE, intuitive astrologer and spiritual teacher

"*Protect Your Light* is a megadeep dive into the wonderful world of energy protection. George covers everything from what it means to be an empath and what is psychic attack to the many ways, wheres and hows of the effects of negative energy. This book contains the most extensive list of protective tools and practices that I have ever seen in one book, so if that's what you're looking for, you will definitely find it here! George also goes into so much detail about how to actually use these protective practices in your life that it's like having your very own spiritual development teacher by your side! A must-read for anyone who is just opening up to spirit and feeling a little hesitant, or those wanting to go deeper and into more advanced energy work."

—VICTORIA MAXWI

T0043146

"This is the clearest, most comprehensive and accessible book on psychic and spiritual protection I have ever seen. Everything is explained simply, and all the questions you want to ask are answered. The exercises and visualizations are easy to follow. I highly recommend this essential guide to making sure your aura is protected."

—DIANA COOPER, author of *Archangel Oracle Cards*

"George Lizos is delightfully talented and a very gifted healer. As we spend more and more time online, it's essential to keep our vibes high and our joy protected. *Protect Your Light* is the answer to your prayers: easy practices to cleanse and shield yourself, both online and offline."

—GALA DARLING, bestselling author of *Radical Self-Love*

"Protect your light, so you can be the light. This book is a first-of-its-kind guide that is here to help us through these intense times and support our well-being. It includes valuable information and exercises for navigating the social media landscape, too. I use George's digital clearing visualizations and techniques regularly and share them with my clients. *Thank you,* George, for writing this book and creating this body of work."

—KATIE BROCKHURST, author of *Social Media For a New Age*

"*Protect Your Light* is the ultimate manual for keeping your energy protected and uplifted. It's filled with practical tools and processes that will help you feel safe in the world, so you can be yourself fully and follow your purpose fearlessly."

—AMY LEIGH MERCREE, medical intuitive and bestselling author of *The Healing Home* and fifteen more books

"*Protect Your Light* is a fearless game changer for navigating spiritual defense. The book is weighty, serving firm resolutions that are both cathartic and freeing. It's an essential for our bookshelves in all spiritual circles."

—CAEL O'DONNELL, author of *Three Minutes with Spirit*

"*Protect Your Light* is the guidebook we all need to embody our highest vibration. In a world where we are constantly on display on social media and vulnerable to absorbing negative energy, light protection brings us back to our innate power. George has a magical way of making this work ethereal while also tangible. He gives us the tools to access our inner lightworker so we can shine brighter for the world. I feel lighter and more magnetic immediately after doing the practices in this book and now have a potent toolkit of light protection practices to use in my daily practice. May we all access this next level of enchantment."

—AMBER-LEE LYONS, host of the *Chakra Girl Radio* podcast

PROTECT
YOUR
LIGHT

A Practical Guide to Energy Protection,
Cleansing, and Cutting Cords

GEORGE LIZOS

Foreword by Diana Cooper

HAMPTON ROADS

Cover design by Leah Kent
Interior by Maureen Forys, Happenstance Type-O-Rama
Typeset in Sabon, Monserrat, Evolve Sans, and Glacial Indifference

Hampton Roads Publishing Company, Inc.
Charlottesville, VA 22906
Distributed by Red Wheel/Weiser, LLC
www.redwheelweiser.com

Sign up for our newsletter and special offers by going to www.redwheelweiser.com /newsletter.

ISBN: 978-1-64297-043-2
Library of Congress Cataloging-in-Publication Data available upon request.

Printed in the United States of America
IBI
10 9 8 7 6 5 4 3 2 1

*To my mum. Thank you for always
supporting me and my dreams.*

CONTENTS

FOREWORD

I was delighted when George Lizos asked me to write a foreword for *Protect Your Light* and immediately sat down to read it. Instantly I was engrossed and could not put it down.

As more and more people wake up spiritually, and as their lights become brighter, it is going to be important to learn how to protect that light effectively.

When I worked as a hypnotherapist, I removed many psychic daggers from people's energy fields, exactly as George describes. I also removed several from my own, but that was many years ago. Something about the way George writes brings up deep "stuff" to be cleared. So I followed the instructions he gives in the Dagger Lifting chapter and immediately remembered someone who used to be very critical of me and who constantly made snide comments. I sensed many small daggers in my energy field from her. Just then, the phone rang, and my attention was diverted. But as I was waking the following morning, I suddenly saw all those tiny daggers join together into one big one! It was a shock. Still, following George's instructions, I worked with the fire dragons and the unicorns to clear all that energy that had been affecting me and felt the relief.

I love working with the different elemental dragons, and the descriptions in *Protect Your Light* are so rich and creative that I could literally feel them coming to me as I read. I laughed when the air elementals, the sylphs, came in as a cool draft wafting through the room, then flowed around me and cleared my aura.

Before I go to sleep, I always ask my fire dragon to place an etheric wall of fire around me, my dogs, and my home, so I was intrigued by George's 360-degree exercise. I scanned around my aura, and sitting firmly in it on my left-hand side was my dragon—big, and fierce, and on duty!

The section on protecting your energy online is immensely important for current times. It is relatively easy to choose television programs, though I have learned to be vigilant ever since I watched one fascinating, but dark, life story. As I watched, black energy started to pour through the TV screen and it was not easy to stop it and clear it. This book made me realize that I need to use one of the protective shields George describes and how much more necessary it is for me to use protection for all pervasive social media. Reading the chapters about the digital world brought home to me how I am inviting all that energy right into my auric field. I shall certainly be using the digital clearing and shielding processes that are so clearly described.

This is the clearest, most comprehensive, and accessible book on psychic and spiritual protection I have ever seen. Everything is explained simply and all the questions you want to ask are answered. The exercises and visualizations are easy to follow. I highly recommend *Protect Your Light* as an essential guide to making sure your aura is safeguarded.

—DIANA COOPER, bestselling author of *The Magic of Unicorns*

INTRODUCTION

You're a sensitive lightworker on a journey to find your life's purpose and live your best life. For as long as you can remember, you've been an empath with an acute ability to pick up on other people's emotions. As a result, your friends, family, and sometimes complete strangers open up to you because they feel safe in your presence, and they know you'll understand and support them.

Your sensitivity has been both a blessing and a curse. On the one hand, the ease with which you can understand and communicate emotions makes you a better friend, parent, partner, and teacher. On the other hand, your sensitivity makes you prone to easily attracting negative energy from people and your environment. You often unknowingly take on other people's problems, absorbing their pain and making it your own. Consequently, you get overwhelmed easily and can't socialize for too long, you also avoid hanging out in large groups of people and need plenty of time to rest and recalibrate following social engagements.

You've often found yourself saying things like this:

I live out in the country and I always feel so overwhelmed when I visit the city.

I feel drained when I take the train during rush hour.

There is this person at work who despises me and I often get terrible headaches after interacting with them.

Sometimes simply standing next to a stranger in line at the store makes me feel inexplicably irritated afterward.

Whenever I chat with this one friend, I feel part of her energy stick to mine.

I almost always feel depleted after visiting a hospital.

I feel suffocated when I chat with certain family members during holiday gatherings.

Using social media used to be a fun way to connect with friends. Now, whenever I log in, I often feel stressed out and depleted.

I got a terrible pain in my stomach after arguing with a person in a Facebook group.

You have a basic energy protection practice, but it's not always effective at keeping you safe. You often sage to clear your aura and house, use crystals to keep your energy high, ask Archangel Michael to protect you, and shield yourself with white light when surrounded by negative people. Although you're confident that the tools and processes you use work, more often you feel that they're not always enough to keep your energy cleared and protected.

You're ready to level up your energy protection practice. You want to understand how energy attack works and learn advanced processes that you can use to both clear and shield your energy. You're ready to go beyond basic, cookie-cutter energy protection processes and adopt a more intricate and personalized approach that safeguards you against external negativity, allowing you to live your life and follow your purpose confidently and fearlessly. Most importantly, you want to be able to use your empathy and intuition to connect with and support others, while still being in control of your energy and knowing that being there for others does not need to come at a cost.

It's my promise that by the end of this book you'll go from feeling unaware of, unprepared to face, or vulnerable to the different types of negative energy to feeling knowledgeable and empowered; you will also have a spiritual toolkit of processes that you can use to clear and shield your energy, both off- and online.

How to Read This Book

Protect Your Light presents a practical, seven-step system for clearing and shielding your energy, so it's important that you read the chapters sequentially. The reason many clearing and shielding processes don't work for many people has less to do with their effectiveness than it does with these people lacking a structured system for dealing with negative energy.

First, not all negative energy is the same, and so different types of energy attachments require you to use different tools and processes to clear and protect yourself from them. Second, our energy field is as complex as the human body, thus managing it requires us to have an in-depth understanding of it. *Protect Your Light* will provide you with a comprehensive understanding of the various types of energy attachments and your energy field and will guide you through a proven formula to clear and protect your energy.

The book is divided into the following four parts:

Part I: Energy Protection Basics discusses the need for energy protection, the symptoms of and vulnerabilities to energy attack, and the seven-step process for clearing, shielding, and strengthening your energy. Additionally, it equips you with the foundational tools of energy protection such as centering, grounding, scanning for energy attack, and connecting to your innate protection power.

Part II: Clear Your Energy introduces a series of practical meditation-based processes for clearing energy attachments. You get to cast a sylph storm, use dragon's breath, take unicorn showers, and create cleansing sacred water potions to clear and purify your energy.

Part III: Shield Your Energy presents the three types of shields, the degree of protection they provide, and guidance on how to layer them for maximum protection. You get to shield and strengthen your energy by bathing in the violet flame, by wearing a golden pyramid of light, by amplifying your energy with the rainbow ray, and by creating your own protective amulets and talismans.

Part IV: Protect Your Energy Online discusses how energy attacks manifest via social media and the digital landscape and provides you with practical energy processes for protecting, clearing, and shielding your online presence.

Since this is a practical book, on many occasions I ask you to take pen and paper and write things down. As a result, it'll be beneficial for you to have a journal dedicated to this journey. Whether it is an electronic or a physical one, the journal will help you keep all the processes in one place so you can keep track of your progress and revisit the practices when you need to.

We're in This Together

I'm fully committed to helping you get to the finish line, and I want to be there for you every step of the way. Here's what you can do to help me support you on this journey:

- Join my private Facebook group community, *Your Spiritual Toolkit.* This is a safe and supportive community of likeminded lightworkers who are all on this journey with you. Use this group to ask questions, contribute answers, and share your journey through the book. I'm actively involved in the group and I'll be there to cheer you on along the way.

- Follow me on Instagram (@georgelizos) and keep me posted on your progress. Send me DMs and tag me in your posts and stories using the hashtag #ProtectYourLight. I read all of my comments and messages and personally reply to everything.

- Download the *Protect Your Light resources* at *GeorgeLizos.com /PYL.* These include a checklist of all the processes in the book that you can check off as you complete them along with downloadable guided meditations of many of the processes.

I look forward to hearing from you and supporting you along your energy protection journey. I have every confidence in you, and I can't wait to see you live your most high-vibe life.

PART I

Energy Protection Basics

CHAPTER 1

What Is Energy Protection?

Take a moment to remember yourself as a child. Without overthinking it, allow yourself to go back to your childhood and get an idea of how life looked then. How did you feel most of the time? How did you spend your time? What were your hobbies and interests? What about your dreams? What was your take on yourself, other people, and the world? Would you say you were optimistic or pessimistic about the future? What were your beliefs about life? Were these mostly positive or negative?

Now, bring your attention back to the present moment and ask yourself the same questions. How are your answers as an adult different? If you're like most people, the way you think, feel, and respond to the world now is miles away from the way you did in your childhood. Somewhere along your path you've strayed from your purely positive, all-loving childhood self, and you've been brought into a world of doubt, judgment, and limiting beliefs.

There are many reasons for this. To begin with, you were brought up in a society based on rules, structures, and expectations. Your parents, the school system, and society at large indoctrinated you with the frameworks of good and bad, positive and negative, right and wrong. You were taught to be a good kid, to play by the rules, and to follow certain systems and formulas that supposedly guaranteed success and fulfilment. You were asked to ignore your intuition and instead trust in other people's expertise and know-how.

As the years went by, new factors were thrown into the mix. You made friends, went to college, discovered your sexuality, got into and out of romantic relationships, had fights and arguments with friends, moved, changed jobs, traveled the world, and so on. In essence, in the period of time between your childhood and the present moment, life got increasingly more complex.

As a result of these complexities, you were exposed to all sorts of energy and you made all kinds of connections to people, places, and things. Each place you've visited, person you've met, and object you've interacted with left an energetic imprint on you that has shaped the person you are today. Just as the ocean shapes the coast and constantly transforms the way it looks, the energetic ocean of your life's experiences has shaped and transformed you.

More specifically, the person you are today—along with your thoughts, beliefs, emotions, and actions—and the reality that you live in this present moment—your job, relationships, health, and general quality of life—are the result of the energetic programming, experiences, and attachments you've been exposed to. Although you may believe that the way you think, feel, and behave right now is who you truly are, the truth is that your authentic self is closer to the one you were as a little child.

In other words, your authentic self is the purely positive, all-loving, and carefree child you once were. When you came into this world, you knew your happiness, worthiness, and loveliness, and you knew what your life's purpose was, too. Your intention coming into this world was to use the knowingness of who you were to create a life that reflected it. Your intention was to think thoughts, feel emotions, and have beliefs that cultivated and expressed your authentic nature. Your intention was to create a career that mirrored your life's purpose and relationships that aligned with your soul's values and beliefs.

If you're not living this life right now, then you're not truly living *your* life; you're living other people's lives. You're thinking other people's thoughts, feeling other people's emotions, having other people's beliefs, following other people's purposes, and enjoying other people's relationships. Essentially, your life has been taken away from you.

Energy protection is about taking your life back.

Defining Energy Protection

I define *energy protection* as the art of being energetically authentic. It's about identifying and clearing what's not yours so you can reestablish your connection with your authentic self and then taking protective measures to secure your authenticity. Energy protection ensures that what's yours is yours, and what's theirs is theirs. It helps you create boundaries between you and the outside world so that you can be in control of the energies that affect you.

Essentially, energy protection helps you live a happier, more authentic, and more fulfilling life. By reacquainting yourself with your inner being, you get to think, feel, and behave from your inner being's perspective. As a result, your entire life changes for the better: you make healthy changes to your lifestyle, you take positive action to improve your relationships, and you take steps to align your career to your life's purpose. Most importantly, you feel safe as you go through life because you know how to secure what you create and protect yourself from unwanted people and energies.

Energy Attack and Energy Attachments

There are various terms that describe the energetic imprints left on our aura when we are interacting with people, places, and objects, as well as their negative repercussions for our health. For simplicity, I'll use the following two terms throughout the book:

Energy Attachments: I'll use this term to refer to all energetic imprints that stain our aura and energy after we interact with our surroundings. Other terms referring to energy attachments include *etheric debris, energy stains, etheric cobwebs, psychic mucus,* and *psychic intrusions,* among others.

Energy Attack: I'll use this term to refer to any adverse effect resulting from energy attachments; this is not to be confused with the term *psychic attack,* which is a specific type of energy attack. You'll learn about the most popular types of energy attack in Chapter 5.

Energy protection is about ridding yourself of toxic energy attachments to prevent an energy attack using the following three steps:

1. **Identify:** Scan your energy and aura to identify the energy attachments staining your energy.

2. **Clear:** Use spiritual processes to clear the energy attachments from your energy to prevent energy attack.

3. **Shield:** Shield your aura using various protective energies with the aim of amplifying your natural auric defenses and warding off incoming energy attachments.

Although these are the three essential steps to energy protection, you'll learn more about four additional steps in Chapter 6.

A Brief History of Energy Protection

Although you probably first heard about energy protection from spiritual books, New Age teachers, Instagram memes, and online spiritual communities, the art of protecting your energy is ancient. Many cultures around the world have used energy protection in one way or another to both clear and protect their energy as well as the energy of their possessions and loved ones.

In ancient times, the primary way energy protection was achieved was through the use of protective amulets and talismans, which you'll learn more about in Chapter 35. In ancient Egypt, the dead were buried with amulets and other tokens to support their journey to the otherworld, and scarabs were placed on the hearts of mummies to protect them against attack in the afterlife. The living employed talismans, amulets—the Eye of Horus and the Girdle of Isis being two popular ones—crystals, and various prayers and incantations to protect against external attack.

In ancient Greece, spells and amulets were used to both curse and protect people from danger and harm. The infamous *curse tablets*, found during Roman excavations in modern-day United Kingdom, were spells written on lead, stone, and wax that were used to ask spirits to perform an action on a person or object, and were thus used as curses. To use these, all people had to do was pay a trained magician to cast a curse or binding spell against their wrongdoers. Aside from utilizing curses, people also often employed amulets—often depicting their intentions, sacred inscriptions, and figures of gods—to protect them from danger and harm.

During the Middle Ages, a proliferation of protective amulets in the form of bones of the saints, pieces of the True Cross, and other artifacts promised to ensure divine protection. Many of these ancient and early-modern protection rituals have persisted. In the Greek-Cypriot Christian culture I grew up in, these bones, alleged pieces of Jesus's cross, protective oils, prayers and incantations, and amulets such as the *nazar* are still used widely to protect against negative people and energies.

The art of energy protection has persisted through time and space in response to the human need for safety and protection. As life and human relationships have gotten more complex, and as our understanding of how energy works has grown, so too has our knowledge of energy protection. The aim of this book is to get you up to speed on the art of energy protection and equip you with what I've found to be the most effective tools, processes, and rituals with which to protect your energy.

CHAPTER 2

Is Energy Protection Necessary?

There are two schools of thought when it comes to energy protection. The first school believes that energy protection isn't necessary. From this perspective, since we're spiritual beings interconnected within a single web of divine consciousness, there cannot be any kind of attack against us. If we know and feel our connectedness with everyone else and the Universe as a whole, then we cannot experience attack, for we cannot attack our own Self.

In other words, this school of thought believes that energy protection subscribes to, and maintains, a belief in duality rather than oneness. Therefore, needing to protect ourselves affirms our ego's false belief in separation from others and the Universe, giving power to fear. Additionally, since our world operates under the law of attraction, putting attention on needing protection from something *attracts* rather than *repels* attack.

From this perspective, the most powerful action we can wield against all forms of energy attack is shifting the way we relate to one another by embracing the notion of oneness. We achieve this by raising our vibration to the frequency of our higher self, who already knows, and vibrates, at the state of oneness.

The Case for Energy Protection

Although I agree that when we're fully connected to Source we cannot experience energy attack, I belong to the second school of thought that considers energy protection an important and necessary practice of daily life.

Here are my reasons.

We Cannot Be Connected to Source 24/7

Yes, when we're connected to Source, we know our oneness and, therefore, cannot be energetically attacked. But, if we were meant to be connected to Source 24/7, then we wouldn't have incarnated into this physical world in the first place; we'd have stayed as immaterial energy consciousness enjoying our connectedness to all that is.

Instead, we made the conscious choice to incarnate in a physical world of duality. We chose to partially disconnect from our oneness and step into our ego—our physical body, hobbies, and personality characteristics. Our aim incarnating as diverse physical beings in a diverse physical environment was to allow for diverse interaction to create more of life and to expand human consciousness.

Yes, our ego believes in separation and, therefore, cultivates fear, but that's why we were born with both the ego and an inner being that's here to correct and guide the ego. All our ego wants is to feel safe and protected, and energy protection is our inner being's way of providing that safety. Locking your door when you leave the house, setting up strong passwords online, and avoiding going out alone at night are all ways of helping your ego feel safe. Why would you treat your energy any other way?

Sometimes, It's Easier to Work with Your Beliefs Than to Change Them

As I mentioned earlier, you get what you believe in. It's how the Universe works. From this perspective, if you don't believe in energy attack, then it can't touch you. Your beliefs are your most powerful protection processes. That being said, if you do believe in energy attack, even if it's a minuscule percentage of your beliefs, then you're vulnerable to it.

When I first started experimenting with energy protection, I was inclined to change my belief about energy attack so that I wouldn't need protection. I soon realized that it was harder to change my belief than it was to work with it. The path of least resistance, in this case, was to accept rather than try to change my belief. Don't get me wrong, there are limiting beliefs that are worth taking the time to release from our consciousness, but this particular one wasn't worth the time for me.

The need to protect ourselves was instilled in us through thousands of years of programming. Since the beginning of civilization, humans have developed ways and processes for protecting their livelihood, and to this day, the industry of protection is a billion-dollar one. Think of all the habits we have, the actions we take, and the systems and technology we use to create a sense of safety. We set strong passwords online, we lock our doors when we go out, we wear warm clothes in winter, and we put sunscreen on when we go to the beach. Our country's legal, military, and police systems are in place to secure our national protection, whereas international politics and military alliances were set up to ensure that all countries coexist peacefully.

The way I see it, our need to protect ourselves is so embedded in our DNA that it's almost impossible to completely deprogram it from our consciousness.

Why Empaths and Lightworkers Need Extra Protection

For these reasons, I believe that everyone needs to clear and protect their energy on a daily basis. That being said, I believe lightworkers need to be extra diligent with their energy protection practice and use more advanced processes, too.

Here's why.

We're More Susceptible to Energy Attack

Because we are more sensitive to energy, lightworkers are significantly more vulnerable to energy attack than most people. As a result, it's easier for us to feel for and receive other people's energy as well as energy in our surroundings. This is a gift in many ways since it helps us to connect with people on a much deeper level. However, if left unattended, this gift can quickly become a liability.

Furthermore, because we naturally see the good in people, we frequently overshare ourselves, both verbally and energetically, with people who may not have our best interests at heart. As a result, we are subjected to more criticism, jealousy, and attack than the average person.

Many people on a spiritual path have come to believe that shielding equals walling themselves off from other people and humanity at large. This couldn't be further from the truth. A *shield* is really a flexible filter that adapts to suit your needs and circumstances. It's a boundary that ensures your light is protected so that you can best use your light with those who need it.

We're Exposed to More Energy Now Than Ever Before

Our world has become increasingly interconnected meaning that we now engage with more people on a daily basis than we did previously both in person and on social media platforms. Simultaneously, an increasing number of people are becoming aware of their psychic skills and the possibility of using energy deliberately. Although most spiritual seekers use their intuitive abilities appropriately, some don't. As a result, it is more crucial than ever to be fiercely protective of our light and energy.

A Lack of Spiritual Training Makes Us Vulnerable to Attack

Often people think that just because they're on a spiritual path and they're doing spiritual work, they're automatically well protected. This is far from the truth. Meditation, healing, self-hypnosis, and all spiritual practices and modalities require training like everything else in life. When most people first start experimenting with spirituality, they usually open up their energy so they have a spiritual experience, but they don't close down afterward because no one tells them they have to.

In truth, it is when you're on a spiritual path and you open up intuitively and energetically that you most need energy protection so you can properly manage energy and navigate the spirit world. Imagine driving a car without the proper training. Sure, you'll be able to drive around without a care for a while, but sooner or later you'll end up getting yourself into some kind of an accident. Managing your experience with spirituality, energy, and intuition works the same way.

Our Purpose Is Too Important

Lastly and most importantly, it's vital for lightworkers to protect our energy because our life's purpose is especially important. As discussed in detail in my book *Lightworkers Gotta Work*, *Ascension Lightworkers* are a special group of old, mature souls who've come to upgrade the Earth's energetic software and help transition our world to the New Golden Age. If you've always had a strong sense of purpose having to do with helping make the world a better place, then you're probably an Ascension Lightworker.

Our collective purpose is vital to helping create the kind, loving world we came here to create. Thus, it's especially important that our energy is truly ours and that it is not affected by external negativity of any sort.

What do you think? Do you see the importance of protecting your energy? Can you see that energy protection is not about subscribing to a belief in fear and attack, but rather it is about acknowledging, and working with, our humanity?

If you see my point but you believe that your connection to Source is strong enough to ensure your protection without additional tools, or if you'd rather work on changing your belief system to deprogram your belief in attack, I still think it's important for you to know how to protect your energy. Having these tools in your spiritual toolkit will help you take action in the rare event that you need to or help you to guide others who need your help.

CHAPTER 3

Symptoms and Vulnerabilities

If you've never cleared or shielded your energy before, or you rarely do so, and your belief system supports the possibility of energy attack of any kind, then your energy is most likely stained by various energy attachments and needs clearing and shielding. (You'll learn more about the mechanics through which your energy field attracts energy attachments in Chapter 4.)

What's important to know about energy attack is that there are different types, expressed in various degrees of intensity, and that they are, therefore, felt and experienced in different ways. We'll talk more about all the different types and the ways of identifying energy attack in your energy in a later chapter, but in this chapter, we focus on recognizing common symptoms of energy attack and the habits and circumstances that make you most vulnerable to it.

By understanding the usual symptoms of energy attack you'll be able to quickly identify when you're being attacked so you can take active steps to protect your energy. Familiarizing yourself with the activities and situations during which you're most vulnerable to attack will help you gauge the degree to which you've been vulnerable over time and help you avoid such circumstances moving forward.

Common Symptoms of Energy Attack

As I mentioned earlier, many different types of energy attack are experienced at various levels of intensity, thus, different symptoms are related to different types of attack. Providing an exhaustive and analytical list of these symptoms would not only require an entire book on its own, but it would also be depressing for all of us! Knowledge is power, but it's never a good idea to focus on the negative side of things for too long.

Therefore I've chosen to share a single list of the most common symptoms of energy attack as a whole rather than focusing on particular types of attack. These symptoms give you a general idea of the degree to which you're affected by energy attack, and you can identify the specific energy attachments causing it in Chapter 5.

Here are the most common symptoms of energy attack:

- Feeling exhausted and fatigued
- Suffering from insomnia and nightmares
- Being oversensitive, beyond what you'd normally expect
- Feeling empty and disheartened
- Lacking interest in daily life
- Experiencing abrupt changes in mood and behavior
- Encountering sudden feelings of anxiety and depression without a known cause
- Exhibiting addictive and obsessive behavior
- Facing a long series of ailments that never clear up after treatment
- Making a series of unexpected mistakes, doing things wrong, experiencing bad luck, and being accident-prone
- Dreading being alone
- Fearing that others are out to get you
- Feeling unable to relax and constantly on edge

It's important to understand that many of these symptoms may be caused by ordinary life situations that have nothing to do with energy attack, such as overworking yourself, enduring long periods of stress and isolation, and experiencing mental conditions and disorders. Be sure to check with your inner guidance before coming to any definite conclusions.

As a rule of thumb, if you experience at least five or more of these symptoms at the same time, then you're likely experiencing a strong case of energy attack; anything between one and four symptoms may suggest a milder case of energy attack. That being said, not having any of these symptoms doesn't mean that you're free from energy attachments or attack. It may simply mean that the energy attachments in your energy haven't yet expressed in energy attack or that you've lived with them for so long that you've become accustomed to them. Unless you clear and shield your energy daily, you are likely to have various energy attachments staining your aura that can express in energy attack at any time.

What Makes You Vulnerable to Energy Attack

Various situations, habits, and activities make you more vulnerable to energy attack, either by weakening and scarring your auric field, by over-stimulating your energy, or by attracting attack from low-level spirits and energies.

Activities and Events That Weaken or Scar Your Energy Field

- Excessive use of tobacco, alcohol, and recreational drugs
- Illness and surgery
- Accidents
- Hospitalization
- Emotional upheaval and sudden shocks
- Addictions
- Assault and violence

- Depression
- Stress and anxiety
- Lack of personal boundaries

Activities and Events That Overstimulate Your Energy Field

- Meditation and hypnosis
- Sudden psychic awakening
- Meddling in psychic activities and modalities
- Use of psychotropic drugs and herbs

With the right training and dosage, all of these activities can be practiced without making you vulnerable to energy attack.

Activities and Events That Attract Energy Attack

- Overconsumption of sensational, drama-filled media such as films, TV shows, newspapers, and magazines
- Hanging out in bars, clubs, and hospitals for too long
- Addictions and codependent relationships
- Using a Ouija board
- Being involved in black magic and dark spiritual arts

To best protect yourself against future energy attack, it's important to avoid extensive use of, and exposure to, these factors as much as possible. If you've already done this in the past, then you've probably made yourself vulnerable to energy attack and your energy field is stained to a certain degree. We work on properly identifying and clearing these energy attachments and attacks in the second part of the book.

Early-Childhood Vulnerabilities

Sometimes, protecting our energy field from energy attack might not be possible because our aura may have been adversely affected in our childhood. When we're born, our aura is not yet fully developed and is engulfed by our parents' auras, particularly our mother's. Consequently, any negative thoughts, emotions, or beliefs that our parents had at the time of our birth and early childhood may have been passed on to us. Additionally, any mental, emotional, or physical issues our parents experienced during our childhood, such as depression, trauma, or serious surgery, may have affected the development of our aura.

When I scan people's energy as part of my psychic clearing sessions, I often see auras that are scarred, have holes, or are thinned out. When I tune in to these vulnerabilities to find out the root cause, I often see early-childhood family drama, mental and physical issues connected to the parents (particularly the mother), and other unstable or traumatic childhood experiences. These early-childhood vulnerabilities hinder the development of the aura, resulting in the attraction of energy attack in subsequent years.

Thankfully, our energy field can always be healed and our auric defenses can be restored. The clearing and shielding processes in Parts II and III of the book will get you started restoring your auric health, but for more serious cases, you may want to work with a psychic clearing professional. You can book a private psychic clearing session with me at *https://georgelizos.com/work-with-me.*

CHAPTER 4

Your Energy Immune System

I n the previous chapter, you learned about the various symptoms of energy attack and the circumstances, situations, and scenarios that allow your aura to become vulnerable to it. In this chapter, we dive deeper into the mechanics of how these vulnerabilities result in energy attack by studying the workings of your energy field, specifically your chakras and aura.

Your chakras and aura form part of your energy immune system, which is as important and is connected to your physical immune system. Your *energy immune system* is responsible for managing your energetic interaction with the people and world around you, filtering and metabolizing incoming energy to protect you from attack. By understanding the mechanics your energy immune system uses to function, you'll be able to more accurately identify energy attachments within your chakras and aura so that you can successfully clear and shield yourself from them.

Your Aura

You are more than your physical body. You have several other bodies that live in parallel dimensions within and around your physical presence. These are usually referred to collectively as an *aura*, or *auric field*.

The *aura* is the life-force energy that pervades both animate and inanimate objects, and its structure is determined by the object's complexity. A human aura, for example, is more intricate than that of a fork or knife, and it can extend up to four feet beyond your physical body.

The human aura has seven main layers corresponding to the seven chakras, which stretch outward from the center of your physical body and into the surrounding world. According to world-renowned energy healer Barbara Ann Brennan, these are the *etheric, emotional, mental, astral, etheric template, celestial,* and *causal bodies,* and they all serve distinct purposes and have various features. Each layer, or body, of your auric field resides within the previous one while expanding progressively beyond the one that precedes it.

Auras can travel between objects, transmitting and receiving energy, due to their fluid and dynamic nature. As you move through life, it is your aura that allows you to perceive the energy of people and places, providing you with ongoing feedback about the world around you. If left unprotected, your aura functions like a sponge, absorbing all kinds of energies from people and locations due to its enhanced perceptive abilities. This sopped up energy remains lodged in your aura unless you intentionally clear it, affecting the way you think, feel, and act in the world.

The first three auric layers are responsible for metabolizing energies related to the physical world, whereas the upper three layers are related to the spiritual realms. The central, fourth layer (astral), which is connected with the heart chakra, is the steering wheel between the physical and the spiritual worlds, managing the transmission of energy between them.

Energy attack tends to manifest within the first three layers, as these are the ones most affected by our daily life and the vulnerability points referred to in the previous chapter. During a conscious or unconscious energy attack, the attacker makes a link to a vulnerability within one of the auric layers, sending negative energy or depleting positive life-force energy. This attack then feeds through to other auric layers, the chakras, and the physical body, resulting in the adverse effects and symptoms of energy attack I mentioned previously.

Your Chakras

Your *chakras* are wheel-shaped energy portals found in specific locations in the center of your body that act as mediums of communication between your physical and spiritual sides. They look like multicolored lotus petals that whirl at various speeds as they transmit life-force energy through the physical, emotional, mental, and spiritual bodies. They're essential to promoting health in mind, body, and spirit.

Your body has seven major chakras, each of which governs a different set of physical, emotional, mental, and spiritual parts of your being. These are the root, sacral, solar plexus, heart, throat, third eye, and crown chakras. Each chakra contains seven layers, which correlate to your aura's seven layers. In my first book, *Be the Guru*, you can discover more about the individual attributes of your chakras.

Any kind of energy attack your aura picks up feeds through to the core of your chakras because the seven layers of your aura are extensions of your seven chakras. At the same time, as conduits between your physical presence and the spiritual, energetic world around you, your chakras have sponge-like properties, absorbing energy from others and your surroundings.

Although each of your seven chakras has its own features and energies and is located in a different part of your body, all your chakras are interrelated. Because all chakras are connected by an energetic channel that runs in a zigzag pattern, an attack on one might impact the entire system.

Your chakras can be blown open by drugs, alcohol, or unsupervised spiritual practices, and they can become stained or clogged when they're overwhelmed with energy attachments. Similarly to your aura, your chakras can also be affected by your parents' negativity in your childhood years. As children, our chakras are wide open with no protective film over them screening out incoming energy. Instead, our chakras are being protected by our parents' energy fields. Therefore, any negative thoughts, emotions, beliefs, or experiences that your parents went through may have been transferred through to your own chakras, hindering their growth and making you vulnerable to energy attack.

If you haven't been consciously clearing and shielding your chakras and aura throughout your life, then all the energy attachments you've attracted over time may still be there, clouding, clogging, and dampening your energy. When I clairvoyantly scan people's energy before they've done any kind of clearing, I often see chakras that are dense and disfigured, clogged with energetic debris and attachments. The colors are dark or pale, their vibrational frequency is low, and the spinning/metabolizing is slow. The uncleared aura usually looks like a dirty, heavy-energy sponge, stained with etheric cobwebs and psychic mucus. The layers don't have clear boundaries; instead they mesh together and interfere with each other's functions and properties. Similar to the chakras, the energy of the uncleared aura feels weak and vulnerable.

CHAPTER 5

Types of Energy Attachments

As discussed in earlier chapters, as you've grown up and lived life, you've been exposed to, and have probably attracted, various forms of energy attachments. If you haven't consciously cleared these, then your energy field is littered with them to one degree or another so that they interfere with the way you think, feel, and behave.

What I haven't mentioned before is that many of the attachments you have may also be related to your lives before the present one—either your past lives or your time in-between lifetimes. During the psychic clearing sessions I do, I often find cords of attachment to people's past lives, to karmic vows and contracts they've made in past lives, and even to spirits and guides they've made agreements with in the spirit world that remain with them in the present time. I also see cords attached to ancestors they've never met, places they've never been to, and experiences they've never had in their current lifetime but that they are still connected to and affected by, via their present-life, ancestral DNA.

You may find yourself wondering how it's possible for something that happened in a past life, or in the spirit world, to affect the way you think in the here and now, especially if you don't have memories of these occurrences. In spiritual truth, we're not just our present lifetime; we're all the lifetimes we've ever lived. Our soul is not limited by this present time-space reality, and it is aware of the totality of experiences we've had in all our past lives and in the in-between lifetimes, too. As a result, the person you are in this lifetime is a cumulative result of hundreds, if not thousands, of past lifetimes.

In this chapter, I introduce the most common types of energy attachments related to both your present and past lives. These are the ones that I see most frequently when I scan and clear people clairvoyantly, and they are the ones that interfere most with our energy.

As you read through the different energy attachment types, it can be easy to let yourself slip into fear and be overwhelmed, so be mindful of that. Remind yourself that you're educating yourself on the subject for the purpose of protecting yourself when you need to. Know and affirm that you are in control of your being, and you're taking active steps to preserve this control. If you start feeling overwhelmed or fearful while reading this chapter, take a break by doing something fun and grounding to come back into your power.

Collective Thought Forms

When a large group of people think similar-feeling thoughts and emotions in a strong and sustained way that's accompanied by action and behavior, they create energetic clouds of these thoughts. These are known as *collective thought forms*, and they linger in the psychic atmosphere of the world looking for similarly vibrational thoughts to attach to. Over time, and as more people contribute such thoughts, these energetic clouds grow in size and power, and start magnetizing people who have a similar vibrational frequency. As people hook into these energy fields, they're fed with an endless supply of similar-feeling thoughts and emotions, causing them to produce even more negativity that feeds back into the thought form. As a result, a vicious circle of negativity is created that sustains the thought forms' control and power.

Each time you find yourself feeling low for an intense and sustained period of time, you become a vibrational match for the energetic cloud of your negative thoughts and emotions, and you risk hooking into the collective thought form. Unless you do something to raise your vibration, you may eventually hook into the thought form and start receiving an endless supply of thoughts, emotions, impulses, and beliefs that amplify your vibrational state.

Have you ever been in a situation in which you suddenly started having an irrational phobia of something? Maybe you've suddenly started to be afraid of flying, or driving on a bridge, or swimming in the ocean. If you reverse-engineer your journey to having that phobia, you'll probably find out that you'd previously practiced an emotion related to the phobia for a sustained period of time. Maybe you've watched one of those dreadful planc-crash movies that has ignited the fear of flying, which you have sustained by having similar-feeling thoughts and emotions, related or unrelated, to flying. As a result, you have hooked into the collective thought form created by all the people who have been afraid of flying in the history of humanity, and you've let that take over.

The power and influence of each collective thought form depends on the degree to which people have practiced its associated thoughts and emotions over time. Certain thought forms are so powerful that they feel and look like raging monsters that scour the atmosphere trolling for people with whom to connect to feed their unending hunger. As a result, they're so easy to be influenced by when your vibration is low, even if you're not hooked into them.

These thought forms tend to have long and tragic histories. Picture the energy surrounding 9/11, the Nazi concentration camps, the world wars, and any other large-scale tragedy. These events have created, and contributed to, collective thought forms that haunt the cities and places in which they occurred. They linger not just in the upper layers of the psychic atmosphere but also in the fabric of daily life, influencing the people who come into contact with them to varying degrees.

Nevertheless, the collective aura of the planet is a reflection of how humanity as a whole has thought and felt over thousands of years. In the same way that there are negative collective thought forms, there are also positive ones that we can connect to just as easily.

Psychic Attack

Also referred to as the evil eye or ill-wishing, a *psychic attack* is when someone directs an intense wave of negative energy toward you, either consciously or unconsciously. This usually occurs when someone feels strong negative emotions toward you, usually anger or jealousy. People who suffer from mental illness, drug addictions, or spiritual possession are also prone to psychically attacking others, although this is usually done unconsciously. Due to the intensity of the energy a psychic attack directs toward someone, it is one of the most serious types of energy attachment. This type of attack usually hurts physically as well as mentally and emotionally, and the symptoms can last anywhere from an hour to days, sometimes weeks.

Psychic attacks tend to be more potent when you have an existing relationship with someone, as the cord of attachment you have with that person gives them access to your energy. However, a psychic attack can also occur between complete strangers and irrespective of spatial boundaries. This is because energy isn't bound by time and space; it can reach anyone and anything as long as there's strong focus and intention.

If you're clairvoyant, you'll probably see psychic attack imprints manifesting as etheric daggers, knives, and other types of conventional weapons on your and others' backs. You may also perceive them as dark masses of energy, cobwebs, or energy stains. These psychic daggers may also be perceived as feelings and sensations, similar to the examples given in Chapter 3.

Karmic Contracts and Curses

Since energy can travel between time and space, and since you're all the lifetimes you've ever had, it's possible that contracts and vows you've made in past lives, as well as curses or psychic attacks you've received, are still affecting you in your present lifetime.

When I scan people's energy, I often see *karmic vows* and *contracts* that look like etheric ties or knots in various locations in a person's energy field. Often, these are contracts of poverty, suffering, victimhood, and celibacy that people made in past lives as a result of their profession, oaths they made, and traumatic experiences. A karmic vow that's common among lightworkers is a vow of suppressing and shutting down intuitive abilities. I often see this as an etheric knot around the third eye chakra, symbolizing a promise many lightworkers made in past lives to reject their intuition and healing abilities, a result of witnessing persecution or being persecuted themselves for working their magic.

I personally made a karmic vow to reject my feminine energy after I had someone stab me in the womb and kill the baby I was carrying in a past life. From that moment onward, I vowed to reject my feminine energy and abuse my masculine energy lifetime after lifetime. As a result, in this lifetime, I almost committed suicide because I couldn't accept my homosexuality (feminine energy), and later on, I kept burning myself out by overworking myself, thus, abusing my masculine energy. You can read the entire story of how I used past-life regression to release this karmic contract in my book *Lightworkers Gotta Work.*

Many karmic contracts are ancestral in the sense that we didn't get to make them ourselves in a past life, but instead we inherited them from our ancestors. Geneticists speak of genealogical karma that includes attitudes, expectations, memories, stories, and contracts that are transmitted down the ancestral line through what's referred to as *junk DNA.* Ancestral contracts create unconscious fears and expectations that an ancestor's fear or intention will be fulfilled, making people feel fearful and hypervigilant for no obvious reason.

Karmic curses are similar to karmic contracts in that they were created in a past life and are still in effect in the present life. The difference is that karmic contracts are usually made voluntarily whereas karmic curses are usually put on you by other people. These curses are psychic attacks that span lifetimes.

Past-Life Traumas

Whereas certain past-life traumas can create karmic contracts, not all of them do. Instead, *past-life traumas* usually create expectations and karmic cords of attachments that we carry with us in our present lifetime. For example, as a result of the multitude of lifetimes during which we've been persecuted as witches, healers, and intuitives, many lightworkers expect rejection and persecution in their current lifetime. As a result, we shy away from sharing our abilities and keep our magic in the closet. These past-life trauma expectations are stored as etheric mucus in our energy field, or cords of attachments to past lives (more on this in a later section) that influence the way we are in the world.

As a rule of thumb, I believe that as soon as a lifetime ends, our energy is reset and we start a new lifetime with a blank canvas. The reason certain contracts, curses, or past-life traumas persist is usually because there's a lesson we had to learn that we didn't get to in the past lifetime, there's a lesson that requires more than one lifetime for us to learn, or we simply didn't have enough time to heal, and find closure from, that specific curse, contract, or past-life trauma in our time between lifetimes.

Psychic Possession

Psychic possession is a serious but rare condition during which a low-level or even an earthbound spirit takes control of a body to such a degree that it results in radical changes of behavior. The symptoms of a psychic possession vary significantly from the symptoms of other forms of energy attack, and they include emotional detachment, strange and destructive behavior, acting completely out of character, memory loss, conversations during which two different voices fight for control, and a bizarre look in the person's eyes.

Possession occurs when there's a severe vulnerability or opening in someone's aura resulting from excessive use of drugs and alcohol, severe exhaustion or burnout, or when someone often abdicates their personal power. This condition is often diagnosed as a mental disorder such as schizophrenia or multiple personality disorder, which may indeed be the case as people suffering from these conditions have little defense against spirit attacks.

Often psychic possession is mistaken for channeling, but the two couldn't be more different. Whereas in psychic possession, a low-level spirit forcefully takes over someone's body through an opening in the aura, *channeling* involves someone with a healthy auric field consciously inviting a loving and benevolent spirit to flow through guidance. With channeling, the spirit doesn't fully or forcefully take over the person's body, but instead, it communicates energy via thoughts, visions, sounds, and emotions.

It's also important to note that despite the frequent portrayal of psychic possession in films and TV series, it's a very rare condition that I've never personally experienced or witnessed. Due to the severity and rarity of this condition, treating psychic possession goes beyond the scope of this book and requires the help of a trained professional. When seeking help with possession, it's important to ensure that the professional you choose doesn't simply banish the spirit but instead moves it on properly or else the spirit will seek out another host.

Psychic Attachment

Psychic attachment is a much milder form of psychic possession during which a living person, a low-level spirit, an earthbound soul, or even an object attaches to a person's aura and influences their behavior. Similar to psychic possession, *attachment* occurs when there's a vulnerability in the person's energy field, such as a break or an opening in the aura, resulting from drug and alcohol abuse, the use of certain prescribed medications, or periods of great negative emotion such as stress, exhaustion, trauma, and depression. This allows an outside entity to hook into a person's aura, sucking away their life force and influencing their thoughts, emotions, and behavior.

I often witness psychic attachment happening in bars and clubs, or wherever there's frequent drug and alcohol abuse. These places are usually packed with low-level and earthbound spirits trolling around for drunk and high humans to attach to so they can feed off of their life-force energy. *Low-level spirits*, also known as *astral entities*, are beingless creatures created from other people's negative thought forms that can only exist when they feed off of a living person's negative energy. *Earthbound spirits* are departed humans that weren't able to fully make their transition, often due to their strong dependency on a habit, substance, or person on Earth, that linger around the Earth plane siphoning the energy of those who're equally dependent on the same vices (i.e., drugs, alcohol, tobacco, fear, stress, depression, codependency, etc.).

In my experience, this form of spirit attachment is very prevalent. In many psychic clearing sessions I've done, I've witnessed, and had to remove, low-level spirits, and sometimes earthbound souls, that were latched onto people's auras, sometimes for years, messing up their psyche. I've personally identified and released multiple entities from my own energy field that I'd attracted during my college years while I was getting drunk and partying in bars and clubs, as well as during my early-life depression and almost-attempted suicide.

Another form of psychic attachment that usually goes unnoticed is one that is caused by owning psychically charged objects. These objects are usually old artifacts that were inherited, purchased, or gifted to you that contain a great deal of residual energy (more about residual energy in the next section), so much so that that energy hooks into your aura and is able to influence your behavior. Remember Tom Riddle's diary in *Harry Potter and the Chamber of Secrets*? That was psychic attachment by an object in full force.

Psychic rape is another type of psychic attachment that's not given much airtime, and yet it's by far the most frequent one. Psychic rape occurs when we have sexual fantasies about another person, or when someone fantasizes about us. Remember that energy travels though time and space, so whenever we intensely fantasize about someone in a sexual way, we channel that energy to them, creating an energetic hook that drains their life force. Someone may argue that because these fantasies occur and stay in their mind, they don't really harm anyone. However, when these fantasies involve a living person, then there's an invasion of someone else's energetic space.

Residual Spatial Energy

As part of my bachelor's degree thesis in Human Geography, I set out to test whether physical space absorbs human experiences and stores them as memory in its ethers, or whether we consciously instill memories in the energy of a physical space using color, symbolism, and performance. To text my hypothesis, I visited Ledra Street in my home town in Cyprus. This street is divided into three distinct spaces, each having a different purpose and use. The first part belongs to the southern Greek-Cypriot part of Nicosia, the second part is in the Turkish-occupied part of the city, and the third and middle part is a neutral zone controlled by the United Nations. That third part is the most interesting one, because it has been left untouched since the 1974 war that led to the Cypriot occupation by the Turks.

To study the three spaces, I interviewed the people walking around in these areas, employed participant observation methods, and also used *psychometry*, the psychic ability of reading the energy of the space to tap into the memories of each part. While walking through the Greek-Cypriot and Turkish-occupied parts of the street, I picked up energies and memories from the people walking by me, energies left there by others who were not currently present, and all the constructed memories built into the street by various bars, coffeeshops, and restaurants. I found myself thinking thoughts and feeling emotions that weren't entirely mine and that were manipulated by brands or that I'd picked up from other people who'd felt a certain way while strolling through the street.

Contrastingly, when I stepped into the UN-managed section of the street and tuned into the energy there, I was almost instantly hit by memories of gunshots and people crying and running away in panic. The 1974 war was playing in a loop in my head—so intensely that I found myself shaking and crying uncontrollably. I had to call it a day!

In my thesis, I concluded that memory is both absorbed naturally by, and is stored in, the ethers of physical space, but it can also be instilled in a space by people and businesses, both consciously and unconsciously. Today, I refer to both of these types of memories as *residual spatial energy*, and I consider them to be the most common and frequent, but also subtle, type of energy attachment.

Each time you move through physical spaces, including your own home, you leave an energetic imprint of the way you feel in the ethers of that space. Simultaneously, you take on residual energy imprints left there by other people or consciously constructed there by brands. At its most severe, residual spatial energy can result in *psychic mugging*, which is when you happen to step into an intense negative residual imprint that someone has left behind. For example, if someone had a huge fight at a certain corner of a street, or someone got murdered there, and you later happened to pass though that corner, you might end up being psychically mugged by the strong energy left there.

Toxic Cords of Attachment

Cords are attachments that you have to people, places, objects, beliefs, or past lives, as well as attachments that others have to you. The degree to which these attachments affect us in a positive or negative way depends on the health and quality of those relationships. When the relationship between two parties is a positive one, there's a pleasant exchange of thoughts, words, and emotions between them, whereas in a negative relationship attachment, there's a toxic exchange of thoughts, words, and emotions, such as anger and jealousy. Energetically, these attachments look like etheric cords connecting the various parties together and facilitating this exchange.

Many people don't think of toxic cords of attachment as a sort of energy attack because sometimes we're the ones who choose to create them. I personally see these cords as one of the most powerful forms of energy attack *because* of this fact. As there is no such thing as an energy attack when we are in a state of oneness and connection with our inner being, it is our ego, not ourselves, that chooses to form a toxic connection to someone or something. Toxic cords of attachment can thus be regarded as self-inflicted energy attacks, making them more difficult to see, acknowledge, and release.

Because they aren't something we pick up on a daily basis, toxic cords of attachment can be the most difficult to deal with and defend against. Rather, these negative connections are the result of the time and effort we've put into fostering relationships with people, places, objects, beliefs, and past lives. As a result, these cords are always connected to us and they feed off of our energy, draining and depleting us. As a general rule, the longer and more intimate the relationship, the stronger and stickier the attachment cord, and the more severe the negative consequences if the connection becomes toxic while the attachment cord remains intact.

Types of Cords

There are many different types of toxic cords of attachment, but the main ones are cords to family members, ancestors, friends and acquaintances, lovers and sexual partners, strangers, pets, places, beliefs, and past lives. Cords of attachment become toxic when the relationship deteriorates in some way, especially when it's become dependent, manipulative, controlling, collusive, or possessive.

Here's how you can recognize the most common types of toxic cords of attachment.

Toxic "Friends" and Acquaintances

Sometimes, the toxic cords of attachments you have aren't related to friendships gone bad but instead to people who camouflage as friends but are really energy or emotional vampires. Usually these people are undergoing deep trauma that's left them feeling unloved and unworthy. Rather than doing the inner work they need to do to heal and grow past it, they instead use other people as their source of light by attaching to them and feeding off of their energy. These are the "friends" that people-please to get closer to you only to inundate you with their constant drama, that never ask about what's going on with you, that constantly ask for your advice but aren't interested in taking it, and that constantly require your attention, support, and encouragement. After your interaction with them, you often feel depleted and exhausted and need a whole day alone to recover.

It's important to have compassion for these people as they're only acting out of their inner suffering, and their dependence is a cry for help. However, you also need to own the fact that you only hang out with them because they help validate and reassure you about something that's missing within you, too. It could be that helping and advising them makes you feel loved, worthy, or needed, or that it satisfies a bigger inner calling to transition to a career that involves empowering others. Before cutting these cords of attachment, it's important to go within and have an honest conversation with yourself about the real reasons you've allowed these people in your life in the first place.

Strangers

It's not uncommon for cords and filaments of attachments to hook into your energy from complete strangers you pass on the street or from people you're connected with online, even if you've never had an interaction with them. If there's a vulnerability in your energy field, people's intentions and energy directed toward you can create a cord of attachment that affects you in a negative way. However, cords of attachment from strangers tend to be weaker than those with people you've had an interaction or relationship with, and they are therefore much easier to release.

Group Cords

In my psychic clearing sessions, I also often see group cords of attachment. These connect three or more people who have shared common experiences, such as a group of friends, a partnership, a group training program, and so on. The way a group cord is laid out mirrors the dynamics and quality of the group relationships so that each member of the group may have various cords extending to smaller groups of people within the parent group cord. Many group cords often involve one main cord asserting control over other people, such as when a group of people depends on a group leader or teacher in online courses and programs.

Depending on the nature of the group cords, they often look like spider webs of various shapes and forms, with energy nodes and filaments managing the nature of the relationships and the exchange of energy between the various parties. Group cords provide an amazing source of energetic support when the group dynamic is healthy and functioning, but when the group relationship deteriorates, or when a number of people within the group cord have a falling out, these tensions can affect the collective energy of the group cord and lead to energy attack.

Lovers and Sexual Partners

Cords to people we've been in long-term relationships with are particularly strong, and when the relationship ends, they can become intensely toxic. Once outlets for communicating loving thoughts and emotions between two people, these cords end up becoming ways of sending anger, resentment, and attack energy toward the other person. The tougher the breakup, and the more unresolved the emotions of anger, resentment, or betrayal, the more toxic and debilitating these cords can be. Even if you're not actively communicating or in touch with the other person, your energetic cords keep the communication channels open and, unless you cut them, these connections can result in energy leeching and manipulation.

No matter how brief an encounter it may be, casual sex also results in cords of attachment. Any intimate physical or emotional contact you have with people requires an exchange of energy. When this exchange is conscious and intent-driven, such as is the case when you have casual sex, you establish a cord with the other person. Although these cords may not be toxic, they allow you each access to the other's energy fields and this can result in energy leeching and psychic rape.

When the sexual encounter isn't conscious or intentional, on the other hand, such as is the case with sexual abuse and rape, a cord of attachment extends from the abuser to the victim that can also lead to energy leeching, manipulation, and psychic rape, thus preventing the victim from healing and moving on.

Pets

Aside from cords to humans, you may also have cords of attachment to pets and animals you have a strong connection with. Although our relationship with our pets is rarely toxic (unless we've been physically hurt by them), it's usually our codependent attachment to them that poses an obstacle for our wellbeing.

Irina came to me after she'd lost a few of her cats to cancer within a short period of time. As you may know if you have or have had a close relationship with a pet, these relationships are equally strong as those with humans, sometimes stronger. The reason Irina was suffering so much even months after losing her cats was because she was unwilling to cut the cords connecting her to her cats' *physicality*. This is an important distinction. The cords she'd had with her cats' spirits were positive ones, and they allowed her to communicate with them in the spirit world. However, she also had attachment cords to the physical presence of her cats in the house, which brought up a lot of pain. After some work, she was able to cut these attachment cords, accept their loss, and transition her relationship with them to a spiritual one.

Places

We have cords of attachment to all the countries, cities, and houses we've lived in. The degree to which these cords are positive or negative depends on the quality of the relationship we've had with these places. However far away we may move from a city or country, unless we cut the negative cords, we'll keep being influenced by both the energy of that place and our negative experiences there. Greek poet C. P. Cavafy expressed this quite accurately in his poem *The City* when he said that *You won't find a new country, won't find another shore. This city will always pursue you.*

When I was nineteen, I left my home country of Cyprus and moved to the UK to attend university. I left behind a painful childhood marked by bullying, rejection, and an almost-attempted suicide, hoping for a new start. Yet, even though I was miles away from Cyprus and the painful memories that came with it, I found myself still engaging in the same habits and suffering from the same fears and limiting beliefs that I'd had while I lived in Cyprus. The reason behind this was the toxic cords of attachments I had to my home island and all my negative experience there. It was only after I consciously cut these cords that I was able to heal and start fresh.

Past Lives

I have been regressing people so they can experience their past lives for over ten years now, and I've come to understand that many of the present-life traumas we have are remnants of past-life traumas. When we experienced something traumatic in a past life, or a number of past lives, and we haven't healed and resolved that trauma, we come into our present life expecting to reexperience it. As a result, we unconsciously create new experiences, particularly in the early years of our lives, to retraumatize ourselves and actualize our expectations.

I often see past-life cords of attachments extending out to the past-life self of the person involved, who also hangs out around the person's aura. If a certain past-life trauma has been experienced repeatedly over many lifetimes, these cords extend out to a series of past lives and past-life selves, creating a powerful group cord of attachment that immobilizes that person's ability to break out of the traumatic pattern.

Past-life cords of attachment often show up as irrational fears and phobias, but also as childhood traumas that, when explored more deeply, are really past-life traumas. By cutting the past-life cords and healing the old trauma through past-life healing and trauma-healing work, you can successfully release the influence of the past and take positive forward action.

Beliefs

In the same way we can have cords of attachment to physical beings such as people or objects, we can also have cords of attachment to immaterial constructs such as ideas and beliefs. Every single belief we have, whether it's positive or negative, is accompanied by a cord of attachment that extends from us into the collective thought form of that belief. As I mentioned earlier, collective thought forms are created by the thoughts, emotions, and energy of all the people who've ever believed in, still believe in, or have contributed to the creation of that specific belief. When we think thoughts and feel emotions related to a specific belief intensely and consistently, we eventually hook into the collective thought form of that belief, which feeds and strengthens our connection to it.

After identifying and cutting these cords of attachment, we often feel energetically freed from the limiting beliefs but can easily reattach to them out of habit. Consequently, what I often do after I help people cut cords to limiting beliefs is to help them create new cords and attach them to positive beliefs that counter the ones they released. This energetic transition eventually feeds through to their mental and emotional bodies, helping them translate the new belief into thoughts, words, and emotions.

Objects

We often have toxic cords to various objects we've had emotional attachments to. These often include family heirlooms, letters, photographs, and gifts that ex-partners, friends, or family have given us. If the relationships to the people associated with these objects ended on bad terms, the anger, betrayal, or resentment you or the other person is feeling is automatically transferred to these objects. Even if you cut your cord of attachment to these people, smaller filaments still connect you to them via these objects. As a result, it's important that you often clear out these items to physically disconnect from them.

What's more, family heirlooms that have been passed down from generation to generation also hold the accumulated energy of all the people who ever possessed them, creating cords of attachments to them and their experiences. It's important to sell, gift, or get rid of such objects, or if you don't want to do that, to clear their energy using one of the clearing techniques in Part II of the book. By physically disconnecting from the objects you have a toxic attachment to, you automatically cut the energetic cord that connects you to them, relinquishing their control over you.

CHAPTER 6

The Seven Steps of Energy Protection

Do you have an energy protection practice but still feel energetically attacked? Do you shield yourself with white light at the start of your day but still feel tired and depleted by the end of it? Do you end up putting so much effort into protecting your energy that it feels like a full-time job?

This is probably because you're not following all, or the right, steps of energy protection. The biggest mistake people make with energy protection is shielding their energy before they take the time to clear it first. Although this protects them from an incoming energy attack, it doesn't clear the existing energy attachments from their energy field. Instead, it shields them in and prevents you from releasing them.

Even if you do take the time to clear energy attachments from your energy field before shielding yourself, you need to take important steps before and after the clearing and shielding process to ensure the protection is lasting and effective. In this and subsequent chapters, you'll learn my seven-step process for protecting your energy and securing your energetic authenticity.

Here's the complete, seven-step energy protection framework:

1. Centering
2. Grounding
3. Connecting
4. Identifying
5. Clearing
6. Shielding
7. Doing the work

We'll cover steps 1 through 4 in this first part of the book, and then we'll continue with clearing processes in Part II and shielding processes in Part III.

CHAPTER 7

Centering and Grounding

The first two steps of the energy protection process are centering and grounding. These underrated practices are, in my opinion, the two most important steps to safeguarding our energy. Mastering these processes will help you take control of your energy so you can safely do the clearing and shielding work later.

What Is Centering?

Centering is one of those spiritual terms that everyone talks about but few understand. I remember reading about centering when I was first starting out on my spiritual path at the age of fifteen. It was almost always used in conjunction with grounding, but I never found a clear definition or explanation of what it really meant, so I went on thinking that centering and grounding were the same thing. In truth, there are clear distinctions between them.

Centering is ensuring that your physical and spiritual bodies occupy, and are present in, the same space. It's about being fully present in your body. As discussed in Chapter 4, our aura has seven main layers. Each auric layer is an entire world of its own, with unique attributes and characteristics, allowing us to perceive the world we live in in different ways. Although these layers are interconnected, they also function independently, letting us perceive through their lenses if we so choose.

When done consciously, we can perceive life through the different layers and dimensions of our aura for the purpose of processing our thoughts and emotions, communicating with our guides, developing our intuition and other spiritual skills, and progressing on our spiritual journey.

However, when we unconsciously or haphazardly shift our perception between these layers, we make ourselves vulnerable to energy attack. How many times have you performed a manual task (using your physical body) while simultaneously thinking about something completely different (using your mental body)? When you did, your physical body was present within a certain task, while your mental body was present in another. In other words, you were in a state of being out-of-place, feeling disconnected or unfocused—all terms used to describe lack of centeredness.

Being uncentered is especially prevalent in modern times, because our attention is constantly pulled in so many different directions. Living in a world of information overload, we're all constantly multitasking, trying to do everything and be there for everyone all at the same time. We go to dinner with our friends and although our body's there, we're on our phones having an entirely different conversation somewhere else. We work out at the gym, and while our body exercises, our mind listens to a podcast. We go on vacation and rather than spend time enjoying every moment, we focus on Instagramming every single detail, thus being in two different dimensions at the same time.

Centering in Energy Protection

Our life, collectively as a human race, is going through a centeredness crisis. From an energetic perspective, we've consciously allowed our auric bodies to function in a disconnected way, not realizing that this makes us vulnerable to energy attack. When our auric bodies aren't present within the same time-space reality for a long time, we're essentially not present within our own being, allowing intruders to attack, influence, or even take over our bodies and energy.

The top four layers of our aura, specifically the spiritual layers, all exist in entirely different dimensions of reality with beings and energies that go beyond the human realm. It is in these dimensions that we can experience angels, our spirit guides, and ascended masters in a more palpable way, but they're also the dimensions in which we can meet lower-level spirits who don't have our best interests at heart. Although consciously accessing these auric dimensions can aid our spiritual journey, when we access them from a place of being uncentered and disconnected from our full presence, they make us vulnerable to attack.

When it comes to protecting our energy, having all our bodies centered and present within the same space reestablishes and strengthens our innate energy protection mechanism. Remember, the most powerful energy protection process is aligning our inner being with our true self. Centering facilitates that alignment but also helps us use other energy protection processes in a mindful way, which is why it's the first step to the energy protection process.

Centering Process

Being centered is your natural state of being, so however much you may have practiced being uncentered in life, it's easy to return back to a centered state. The following process is the one I've used for years to center my energy. You can use it anytime you feel as if you're lacking a sense of presence and focus and also as the first step to your energy protection practice.

Here are the steps to the process:

1. Sit comfortably and close your eyes.
2. Take long deep breaths through the nose, taking the air down to your belly, and then exhaling fully until your lungs are empty.

3. While breathing, focus on relaxing your physical body. Start from the top of your head, and progressively move down through all parts of your body, gathering up stress and tension with the inhale and releasing it with the exhale.

4. Once your body is fully relaxed, use your mind's eye to get a sense of your emotional body, the second layer of your aura. This layer is your emotional center, so accessing it essentially involves getting a sense of the way you feel. With each breath, just concentrate on any emotions you're feeling and let them be. Acknowledging them is enough to center your emotional body.

5. Move on to the mental body of your aura, the third layer, and follow the same process. Simply acknowledge the thoughts that come up in your mind, and then let them be.

6. With your mind's eye, visualize the remaining four layers of your aura collectively. These are the spiritual layers and they aren't as easy to access as the first three. However, all that you need to do to bring them into a centered state is to keep breathing while you visualize them taking their natural position around your physical body.

7. Once you've mindfully acknowledged the seven layers, or bodies, of your aura, focus your attention in the center of your heart and visualize your heart chakra magnetizing all seven layers toward it, as they energetically hook into it. As the connecting point of your physical and spiritual bodies, your heart is the steering wheel of your centeredness, so hooking your auric layers to it secures this state.

8. Once you feel present, centered, and focused, take a few more deep breaths and open your eyes.

What Is Grounding?

Whereas centering is about ensuring that your physical and spiritual bodies occupy, and are present in, the same space, *grounding* ensures that your being, with all its various bodies, is firmly present in, and connected to, the Earth. Centering is a prerequisite to grounding, as to be consciously present in, and connected to, the Earth, you (the whole of you) need to be in the present moment, which is what centering helps you achieve.

The reason we refer to our planet as Mother Earth is because, from a metaphysical perspective, our planet is our mother. If it weren't for the Earth, we wouldn't be who we are today. Our planet provides the platform from which all life originates, and without it we'd just be immaterial Source Energy consciousness. Our biological mother may have brought us into this world, but that's only because there is a world in the first place.

The ancient civilizations of our world knew this deeply, and so they honored, respected, and lived in partnership with the Earth. Before the rise of modern, man-made religions such as Christianity, Islam, and Judaism, the dominant religion and spiritual tradition in many cultures around the world was paganism, an Earth-based spiritual tradition. What distinguishes paganism from modern religions is that it's based on honoring and living in alignment with the Earth's natural cycles, and also seeing Source in everyone and everything, including the Earth. As a result, the act of grounding was etched into the very framework of religious and social life. This is in contrast to the ways of modern life and religion, in which Source is seen as disconnected from the Earth and is often perceived as something abstract and distant from daily life.

Grounding in Energy Protection

In the same way we have energetic cords of attachment connecting us to our human mother and to other people in our lives, so too do we have a cord connecting us to the Earth. Unlike the human cords that can be consciously severed when a relationship isn't working, our Earth cord can only be severed when we make our transition back into Source.

That being said, although our connection to the Earth can never be severed while we're still alive, it can certainly be weakened. When we're uncentered and spend much of our time outside of our physical bodies, our Earth cord of attachment weakens, leaving us feeling disconnected from the physical world around us. During sleep, visualization, or a guided meditation, for example, you consciously unground yourself so your body can rest or you can have a spiritual experience. But, right after sleep or meditation, you're usually instinctively guided to drink some water, have something to eat, or do something physical to reestablish your connection to the Earth.

Conversely, being ungrounded in an unconscious way can make you vulnerable to energy attack. When you're consistently disconnected from the Earth, you essentially disconnect from your own body and physicality. This not only messes up your alignment with Source and your inner being, but it also leaves your body exposed to the spirit world and other external energies. As a result, your natural energy protection mechanisms are weakened, which makes you vulnerable to energy attack.

When you take the time to consciously ground your energy and strengthen your cord of attachment to the Earth, you align fully with your body and inner being, sending out a signal that you're at home in your body and on the planet, and that your energy is intact—and will stay that way.

What's more, grounding is a powerful clearing and shielding process in and of itself. Your Earth cord has two energy tubes, one aimed at flushing out negative and excess energy, and the other for replenishing your body's life force from the Earth's inexhaustible reserves. Thus, grounding is at the basis of energy protection because it's the foundational power source of your energy immune system.

The Grounding Process

You can use many processes to ground yourself, many of which are as simple as walking barefoot out in nature, having something to eat, or just clapping your hands together a few times. However, for the purpose of energy protection, it's important that you ground yourself more deeply and consciously. Use the following meditation process to ground yourself after you've gone through the centering process in the previous section.

Here are the steps to the process:

1. Sit in a meditative state and close your eyes.

2. Having centered yourself, concentrate on your root chakra, which is at the base of your spine. You can visualize it as being a bright ball of ruby-red light. Your root chakra governs your connection to the Earth and the physical world around you, and it is your main chakra to work with for grounding.

3. Visualize a cord of attachment extending from your root chakra down into the Earth below you. Let this cord dig deeper into the Earth, passing through various layers of soil, through caves and crystal mountains, and crossing the threshold of the Earth's crust into the magma until it reaches the Earth's core.

4. Let this cord tie itself around the Earth's core, which looks like a giant red crystal, very similar to what your root chakra looks like.

5. Having tied yourself around the Earth's core, visualize all stress, tension, and negativity flushing out of your various bodies through this cord, into the Earth, letting that energy be recycled by Gaia. Simultaneously, let healing, grounding energy from the Earth stream up this cord into your physical body, energizing and grounding you.

6. Stay in this position for as long as it feels right, and when you're done, take deep breaths in and open your eyes, feeling great and grounded.

Centering and grounding yourself are the two most essential steps you can take to strengthen your natural energy protection mechanism and to prepare for actively clearing and shielding yourself from energy attachments. In the next chapter, we dive into the third step of the energy protection process, which involves connecting with your power to clear and protect.

CHAPTER 8

Connecting to Your Protection Power

*Y*ou are your most powerful tool for energy protection. All the tools, processes, techniques, and meditations you'll learn about in this and other books are only as powerful as your own protection power. More specifically, your physical body and intention are all you need to both clear and shield yourself; all other processes are complementary.

The reason we use tools and processes for energy protection, or for any spiritual endeavor, is partly because it's fun to do so but mostly because we expect to receive more value through physicality. The reason we incarnated in this diverse physical world, versus staying in the spirit world, is that we wanted to express our creativity and Source Energy consciousness in a physical and practical way. Our physicality, then, affords us an inevitable dependence on physical objects, tools, and processes.

Concurrently, although we know we're a part of, and extension of, Source, and we understand that we can call upon the essence of Source as a whole for protection, we enjoy compartmentalizing Source into a diversity of spiritual beings, such as gods, goddesses, and elementals, because it's easier for us to work with it this way.

As you go through the processes in this book, learning about different techniques and connecting with various spirit guides, keep reminding yourself that these beings and processes don't really offer you something you can't offer yourself. They're extensions of your own protection power, and they are only as effective as you allow them to be. At the same time, the spiritual beings you connect with aren't separate from you as we're all part of the same Source Energy consciousness. They're simply different expressions of Source, and therefore of you, helping you access certain energies and qualities that you already have in an easier way.

Meditation to Step into Your Protection Power

Before we dive into the clearing and shielding processes part of the book, it's important to fully embody your protection power; the following meditation will help you do so.

Here are the steps to the meditation:

1. Close your eyes to come into a meditative state, and go through the steps of centering and grounding your energy as explained in Chapter 7.

2. Focus your attention on your solar plexus chakra. Your solar plexus is the doorway to your personal power. It metabolizes the protective energy of Source through your being, awakening your inner strength, confidence, and willpower, helping you feel safe within your body and in the world.

3. Visualize your solar plexus chakra being a tiny ball of yellow light in the center of your solar plexus area, growing larger with each breath you take. See this golden ball of light expand until it fills up your entire body and extends out into your aura. When this happens, you'll feel your vibration rising, your life force

increasing, and your natural protection power flooding your entire being.

4. While in this state, affirm the following statement three times, mentally or out loud: *I step into my power to protect myself. I'm centered in my energy and grounded to Earth. I'm safe and secure.* Stay in this state for as long as you need to feel uplifted and invincible.

5. When you're done, take deep breaths in and gradually come out of the meditation.

You can download an expanded audio recording of this meditation at *GeorgeLizos.com/PYL*.

Your Energy Protection Guardian

Having fully embodied your innate protection power, you're now ready to expand that further by connecting with your *energy protection guardian*. This is a personal spirit guide you can choose to connect with to support you through the clearing and shielding processes to come. Your energy protection guardian can be an existing spirit guide you work with, such as a guardian angel or an elemental guide, or it can be any new spirit guide that wants to make contact with you, such as any other angels or elementals, an archangel, ascended master, a god or goddess, or any other benevolent deity you choose to work with.

Think of your energy protection guardian as an extension of your innate energy protection power that acts as your advocate in the spirit world. The guardian is responsible for connecting you to other guides you wish to call on for protection, guides you to choose the best clearing and shielding tools, sustains the effectiveness of your energy shields during the day, and even acts as your energetic bodyguard when your natural energy defenses are weakened. Once you meet your energy protection guardian, they'll be with you at all times (as long as you want them there), guiding, supporting, and protecting you.

Use the following meditation to meet your energy protection guardian:

1. Close your eyes to come into a meditative state. Go through the steps of centering and grounding your energy as explained in Chapter 7.

2. Put in your request to the Universe to meet your energy protection guardian by mentally or verbally saying, *I call upon my personal energy protection guardian to come into my presence and show up in a way that I can experience them clearly.* As soon as you say that, let go of expectations and stay still, breathing deeply and noticing who shows up. Depending on your dominant intuition language, you may experience your energy protection guardian visually, mentally, emotionally, or auditorily. (Refer to my books *Be the Guru* and *Lightworkers Gotta Work* to find and strengthen your main intuition languages.)

3. When your guardian shows up, spend some time getting to know them in the same way you would a new friend. Be sure to ask them why they chose to work with you and give you guidance as to what you can do to strengthen your natural energy protection defenses.

4. Before you end the meditation, ask your energy protection guardian to stay with you as you explore the processes in this book and to guide your daily energy protection practice. You'll learn a specific process for working with your energy protection guardian in Chapter 36.

You can download an expanded audio recording of this meditation at *GeorgeLizos.com/PYL.*

CHAPTER 9

It's All Attraction

When learning about the various ways other people, objects, places, and past lives can affect our energy, it can become easy to see ourselves as the victims and blame anyone else but ourselves for our feelings, circumstances, and misfortunes. A lesson that's tough but necessary to learn on your journey to protecting your energy is that in spiritual truth, there's no such thing as assertion; it's all attraction. In other words, nobody has the power to assert a negative or positive experience in your life unless you're a vibrational match to it.

I've touched on this in earlier chapters, but it's worth revisiting and taking a step further. One of the most powerful law in the Universe is the *law of attraction*, which states that like attracts like. The law of attraction responds to our vibrational frequency, and therefore the way we feel, which, in turn, is influenced by the thoughts we think and the words we speak. Put simply, we attract things, people, and experiences that are a vibrational match to the way we feel. From an energy attack perspective, we can only attract energy attachments if our vibrational frequency, the way we feel, matches the vibrational frequency of the energy attachment.

Since we are the ones attracting all energy attack, the real work in energy protection has to do with doing the inner work of identifying the root causes behind what we attract and taking action to heal and resolve them. In my experience in working with people over the years, I've identified three main root causes behind energy attack: unresolved traumas, limiting beliefs, or chronic negative thinking.

Unresolved Traumas

When I first started learning about and practicing energy protection, I fell into the trap of feeling victimized and thinking that everyone was out to get me. Whenever I met someone new, hung out with a group of people, or visited a crowded place, I'd later come home and identify dozens of psychic daggers on my back. As I strengthened my clairvoyance and began to see these daggers more clearly, however, I realized they were self-inflicted rather than sent to me by others.

Perplexed, I dug deeper to identify the root cause of what I experienced. After some soul searching, I concluded that I'd still had an unresolved fear of judgment and bullying stemming from my childhood. Growing up gay and different, I experienced a great deal of bullying, not just from others but also from myself. As a result, I came to expect judgment and attack from people. Even though I'd done a lot of work to heal that childhood fear and have even written two books about it, some part of it was still active within me so that anytime I met someone new, I still unconsciously expected to be rejected and attacked. Ever since I made this realization, I have noticed a significant drop in the number of psychic daggers on my back.

With this in mind, before you clear energy attachments, observe them with a curious mind. Look beneath the surface for past unresolved traumatic experiences that may have created a false sense of attack. An easy way to do this is to identify the negative emotion produced by an energy attachment and then ask yourself, *When was the first time that I remember feeling this emotion?* This allows your mind and body to search for past traumatic memories that may have contributed to your potentially perceived attack. If memories do come up, explore them through the journaling exercise at the end of this chapter to gain a deeper understanding.

If nothing significant comes up, you may indeed be experiencing energy attack.

Aside from producing a false sense of attack, our unresolved traumas can also attract an actual energy attack. Our past traumatic experiences inform the way we perceive ourselves, other people, and the world around us, thus shaping our thoughts, emotions, and beliefs. As a result, unresolved traumas usually create long-standing limiting beliefs that lower our vibrational frequency and attract people and circumstances that both validate and add to what we feel and believe.

By doing the inner work to identify and release past traumatic experiences, you automatically eliminate perceived energy attack and also reduce the number of real energy attack you attract.

Limiting Beliefs

Self-sabotage occurs when the beliefs and desires we have about ourselves haven't caught up with the beliefs and desires that our higher self has for us. As a result, when an opportunity for growth, happiness, and fulfilment shows up in our life, our ego comes in to sabotage it. Usually, self-sabotage comes in the form of excuses and limiting thoughts about ourselves, other people, and life in general. As a result of our self-sabotaging beliefs and the subsequent excuses they create, we inevitably attract to us energy attack that give us an easy way out. We can then lie to ourselves by claiming it wasn't our fault that things didn't work out because other people were out to get us or we had a streak of bad luck.

Self-sabotage is particularly strong with lightworkers because our collective purpose extends beyond our personal wellbeing to the wellbeing of the entire world (you can read more about this and how to find your life's purpose in my book *Lightworkers Gotta Work*). As a rule of thumb, the bigger our life's purpose is, the stronger the ego's self-sabotaging strategies will be. I see self-sabotage camouflaged as energy attack a lot within the online courses and workshops I teach. Often, people sign up for a course excited to take a leap in their personal growth and development only to face overwhelming "coincidental" drama at some point during the course that prevents them from finishing it.

Usually, self-sabotage is rooted in a single core limiting belief we have about ourselves that creates further minor beliefs that the law of attraction responds to. Drama queens/kings are prime examples of how this works. You recognize drama queens/kings as the people in your life with whom you spend hours on the phone, counseling and giving them support, but they never take your advice. These people tend to have one dramatic problem after another, and as a result, they are the perfect victims of energy attack. On the surface, it seems as if their daily debacles are the result of a series of bad choices, negative thinking, and limiting beliefs. In truth, these are just the result of a single core belief that was probably created early on in their life, and it ended up catching on and has wreaked havoc ever since.

Chronic Negative Thinking

Chronic negative thinking can be the result of unresolved trauma and a root cause belief, or it can be simply a habit we practiced for so long that we don't know how to break out of it. In either case, chronic negative thinking creates chronic negative emotions that lower our vibrational frequency and make us a match for an array of energy attachments. It's not hard to fall down the rabbit hole of negative thinking because we live in a world that glorifies it. You only need to watch the news consistently for a week and you'll end up believing that people are out to get you, that your dreams will never come true, and that our planet is dying. Moreover, the popularity of reality TV, gossip shows, and drama-filled movies and TV shows further proves how we live in a world that thrives on drama and negativity.

According to Bessel van der Kolk, author of *The Body Keeps the Score*, once the body adjusts to a certain uncomfortable or dramatic situation, it eventually comes to crave the drama. In this text he writes: "This gradual adjustment signals a new chemical balance has been established within the body. . . . Just as with drug addiction, we start to crave the activity and experience withdrawal when it's not available. In the long run people become more preoccupied with the pain of the withdrawal than the activity itself."[1]

Since it's so easy to get caught up in chronic drama and negativity, it's inevitable that the resultant lower vibrational frequency will attract a series of energy attachments from people and places. This is the reason so many spiritual teachers emphasize the importance of having a daily spiritual practice; it helps us disrupt our chronic negativity and start building a positive momentum of attraction instead.

Doing the Inner Work

Now that you know that you're responsible for attracting all energy attachments and are familiar with the three main root causes behind them, it's time to do the inner work of identifying and releasing them. The easiest way I've found to do this is a process I call *The Five Whys*. This process encourages you to identify the emotional response behind an energy attachment and then ask yourself why you feel this emotion five times. In my experience, by the fifth time you ask yourself why you feel a certain way, you end up with the core limiting belief behind this. This limiting belief could fall into one of the three categories mentioned earlier, or it could be something different.

Here's an example of how this works:

Let's say you've identified a psychic dagger on your back. Before you clear it, take some time to tune in and consider how having this dagger makes you feel.

It makes me feel angry.

Then, ask yourself *why* five times, answering the question intuitively and without overthinking it.

Why does it make me feel angry? Because I don't know who sent it to me, or why.

Why does it upset me that I don't know who sent it to me?
Because I don't know who to trust.

Why do I need to know who to trust? Because this way I'll be
able to protect myself from toxic people.

Why do I need to protect myself from such people? Because I
don't feel safe in the world, and keeping away from them will
help me feel safer.

Why do I not feel safe in the world? Because my mother left
me alone for hours when I was a child. I was lonely, scared,
and felt unsafe.

In this example, the core belief behind the psychic dagger and the subsequent emotion of anger is an unresolved trauma, specifically parental abandonment. When this core issue is identified and healed, all subsequent limiting beliefs that were created as a result, including the triggered emotion of anger and the psychic dagger that was either attracted as a result of this belief or was just a perceived form of attack, will be gone.

There are many processes for healing and resolving the core beliefs behind your energy attachments. You can go to therapy; use the Emotional Freedom Technique (tapping) or Integral Eye Movement Therapy (IEMT)—something I do in my personal practice; practice inner child meditations; cut cords, which you'll learn about in Chapter 24; or simply journal about your emotions to transmute them into more positive ones. Always consult with your inner guidance to take appropriate action toward healing and releasing these core limiting beliefs and work with people and processes that you feel drawn to.

Doing inner work is by far the most powerful step you can take toward protecting your energy. The more work you do to identify and release your core limiting beliefs, the higher your vibration will be, and the fewer energy attachments you'll attract. As you heal and release your core beliefs, you'll strengthen your natural auric defenses to such an extent that you'll barely need additional energy protection processes.

CHAPTER 10

The Power of Intention

As I mentioned in Chapter 2, when you don't believe in the existence of energy attack you can't be affected by it. Your conviction projects a powerful intention of always being protected and aligned to Source, which automatically casts all the protection "spells" you need to keep your energy cleared and shielded.

Similarly, when you use the energy protection tools, processes, and meditations in subsequent chapters, it's your *intention* behind using them that will clear and protect your energy, not the actual processes themselves. If you take your focused intention out of the equation, you rid the processes of their power and effectiveness.

When you set out to try these processes, always take some time to center and ground yourself, and step into your power using the meditations described in previous chapters. See yourself aligned to Source and focus on your intention of clearing or protecting your energy. Then, and only then, will you be able to start using the suggested processes effectively.

The Law of Free Will

You'll be encouraged to call on spiritual beings in a few of the clearing and shielding processes that follow. Although it can be tempting to give your power away to these guides that seem external to, and more powerful than, you, it's important that you don't do so.

First, keep in mind that these beings are not separate from you, just as you are not separate from anybody or anything else in the Universe. We're all one in spiritual truth, including angels, elementals, spirit guides, and ascended masters. When you connect with these guides, you're simply connecting with a larger version of yourself.

Second, these guides can only assist you if you grant them permission; hence, obtaining assistance is also contingent on your intention. Spiritual beings can only aid you if you give them access to your energy, according to the law of free will. Yes, you are connected and one with them in spiritual truth, but you chose to incarnate as a distinct physical entity in this lifetime because you desired the freedom to do as you pleased.

When you have to call on these spirit guides, make sure you mentally set your intention and grant them permission to assist you while also understanding that you're receiving assistance from a higher, extended part of yourself. This will guarantee that you do not become reliant on these beings for help and protection but rather call on them as and when necessary.

Setting Clear Intentions

Although I am confident that you are aware of the importance and power of your intention in clearing and protecting your energy, you may be unsure of how to effectively communicate your intention.

In the processes that I'll guide you through in the following chapters, you may wish to express your intention in one or more of the following ways:

- **Visualization:** This is imagination that is focused and deliberate. You may be instructed to visualize light, etheric cords, or spiritual beings throughout some processes. The very act of coming up with an image in your mind establishes your intention to work with these sources of light, energy, and beings.

- **Thoughts:** If you're not a visual person, you can think about or will these processes to happen in your head. Rather than visualizing light all around you, you may simply think about it. Your thoughts and visualizations are equally intent-laden.

- **Words of Affirmation:** The third technique for using intent to activate these processes is to simply say out loud what you wish to happen. Make up a simple affirmation like, *I shield myself with protecting rainbow light intending for it to stay with me throughout the day and protect me from all negative energy and people.*

- **Written Words:** Writing things down in your notebook, in a computer document, or on a piece of paper is the final way of expressing your clear intention for clearing and protection. When you write anything down, it becomes real. When we spend too much time in our heads, our focused intentions can become lost in the noise. We separate our intentions from the rest of our thoughts when we write them down, giving them more strength.

If it helps you focus, you can use any combination of these four ways. You can visualize yourself surrounded by light while thinking, writing, and verbally affirming its protective qualities.

CHAPTER 11

Identifying Energy Attachments

Before you attempt any clearing or shielding processes, it's important to first know what you're dealing with. Identifying energy attachments is the fourth step to the energy protection process and it involves using your primary intuition languages to identify the types of energy attachments that we discussed earlier within your energy field.

If you've never cleared your energy before, you'll almost certainly come across a lot of energy attachments that need to be released. Don't be alarmed or scared by this; in the next chapters, you'll learn how to effectively release all of them.

Scanning and clearing your energy for the first time will most likely require a significant amount of time and effort, but after you're done, you'll be able to complete the process in less than ten minutes a day. Every morning, as part of my spiritual practice, I scan, clear, and shield myself. It's become as much a part of my everyday routine as brushing my teeth and putting on my clothing. I've observed noticeable changes in my energy and wellbeing since I started doing this.

Turn On Your 360-Degree Vision

You must first activate your intuition before you can begin scanning for energy attachments. There are a variety of methods for doing so, but my personal favorite involves a technique that my spirit guides taught me early on in my spiritual path. It entails activating my 360-degree vision.

Although your physical eyes are limited in their ability to observe the world around you, your spiritual bodies are multidimensional and can perceive all directions at once. The following technique helps you to change your focus from the physical to the spiritual realms, which activates your intuition and allows you to sense energy attack much more clearly.

To activate your 360-degree vision, follow these steps:

1. While meditating, concentrate on your third eye chakra, which is located between your brows in the center of your head. Your third eye chakra is your intuition's control tower, allowing you to change your focus from the physical to the spiritual planes. Imagine your third eye chakra as a vivid purple ball that swells larger with each inhale. Deeply breathe until you notice a shift in your energy as your third eye chakra expands.

2. Now that you've opened your third eye chakra, you can begin to awaken your 360-degree vision. Visualize what's there in front of you without opening your eyes. Use your mind's eye to get a feel for the energy dimension of the physical environment before you. Don't second-guess yourself or overthink this. Simply be aware of what's coming up.

3. Maintain your inner vision of what you're seeing in front of you while expanding your vision to include what's on your right and left so you can see everything at once.

4. Next, increase your field of vision so that you can see what's above and below you as well as what's in front of you and to your right and left.

5. Finally, broaden your vision so that you can see what's behind you while also seeing what's in front of you, to your right, left, above, and below. Stay in this awakened state for a few minutes and allow your body to acclimate to your newfound 360-degree vision.

Psychic Scanning Process

Having awakened your psychic vision, you're now ready to scan your body for energy attachments. As soon as you've finished turning on your 360-degree vision, use the following scanning method:

1. With your 360-degree vision turned on, focus on your physical body to see its energetic dimension and the first layer of your aura, known as the etheric body. Look for psychic daggers, collective thought forms, or residual spatial energy in the form of dark energy, vibrational stains, and etheric cobwebs. Keep in mind that depending on your primary intuition language, you may not be able to see these, but rather you may experience them through a different sense.

2. Examine your etheric body more closely to see if there are any toxic cords of attachment going outward toward other people, items, places, beliefs, or past lives. Many of these cords will be connected to your chakras, particularly your heart and solar plexus. Are these cords that you have created or that others have attached to you? By mentally "touching" the cords and paying attention to how you feel, you can get a sense of this. This will help you better understand the relationship and nature of the attachment.

3. Shift your focus away from the toxic cords and concentrate on your seven chakras. What do they appear to be like? Are they bright and clean, or dark and dingy? What would you say about their health? Are any psychic daggers penetrating them, or are

dark energies clogging them? What types of energy attachments, if any, do you see there?

4. Finally, expand your awareness to observe the layers of your aura that extend all around you. You might notice dark stains of energy, low-level spirits, residual spatial energy, or other bad vibes that your aura has absorbed over time in this area. Simply look at them without passing judgment.

5. When you've finished scanning for and identifying energy attachments within your body and aura, come out of meditation. Make a note in your journal of what you've discovered so you can either clear it later or continue on to the processes in the following chapters.

You can download an expanded audio recording of this meditation at *GeorgeLizos.com/PYL.*

PART II

Clear Your Energy

CHAPTER 12

Partnering with Nature for Protection

" plan to use these skills in succeeding to my prime aim, which is to improve international environmental policy and make sustainability the world's major concern." This is how I concluded my personal statement when I applied to universities to do a bachelor's degree in geography at the age of nineteen. Like many lightworkers, I was distraught by the environmental destruction we've inflicted on the planet over thousands of years and wanted to dedicate my life's work to saving the Earth.

Surprisingly, I wasn't long into my degree when I realized that my premise was slightly problematic. Immersing myself into the history and geography of our planet, learning about plate tectonics, volcanoes, atmospheric processes, and ocean currents, I was amazed by the power of the Earth to regenerate despite the destructions it has endured. These powerful natural processes are constantly at work, flushing out impurities and creating new life; sustaining the vitality of the planet and creating the perfect environment for its thriving. As a volcano erupts on one side of the world, a tectonic plate plunges into the magma somewhere else, balancing the forces of creation and destruction, both physically and energetically. In the same way, atmospheric phenomena, such as storms, tornadoes, and hurricanes, earthquakes, glacial movements, soil systems, and ocean currents all follow the same processes of creation and destruction to rid the Earth of impurities and to sustain its vitality.

The evidence of these processes' success is in the longevity of planet Earth. In the 4.543 billion years it has existed, the Earth has been through all sorts of changes and environmental destructions, and it has always come out a winner. For the two to three hundred thousand years that modern humans have existed on the planet—which is a blink of an eye in the Earth's timeline—the planet has continued to thrive, wiping out the civilizations that abused her and maintaining her balance no matter what. Yet, here we are thinking it's *our* responsibility to save the planet . . .

Don't get me wrong, I'm all about loving and respecting our planet and doing everything we can to curb pollution and transition to sustainable development and lifestyle. However, knowing what I know about the history and geography of our planet, it feels arrogant to think that we have the power to save it. I've come to believe that our collective human purpose has less to do with saving planet Earth and more to do with saving the human race. Whereas the Earth has survived all possible destructions for over 4.5 billion years, many human civilizations haven't even lasted a fraction of that time. Who's to say the Earth won't just wipe us out if we keep abusing her?

The Greatest Protector

The reason I'm going to such great lengths to stress the power of our planet to heal and thrive is to show that the Earth, Lady Gaia, is the most powerful energy protector there is. In fact, she's the first energy protector that ever existed. She's the OG! The Earth's destructive processes are clearing agents that cleanse the Earth of toxic energy attachments, and her creation processes are shielding agents that bring forth life-force energy and keep raising her vibrational frequency. We have so much to learn about energy protection simply by connecting with the powers of nature.

After I received my undergraduate degree in geography, I began connecting with and studying the Earth from a spiritual perspective, too. I partnered with nature's wisdom by connecting with the nature beings—the elementals of earth, air, fire, water, and spirit; the gnomes and fairies; the sylphs, dragons, mermaids, and unicorns. Aligning with their energy and wisdom has allowed me to use the same processes that nature uses to restore her balance to clear my own energy and return to my balance, too.

Today, I'm sharing these processes with you in this book. Although I've included many different processes for clearing and shielding your energy, the majority of these processes involve partnering with nature's wisdom. Yes, there is wisdom in the stars, in other planets, in angels and ascended masters, but why search for wisdom outside of our planet when we can learn so much here? I believe that all the answers we seek are in nature, and when we take the time to honor, respect, and learn from her, she'll give back abundantly.

Connecting with the Elementals

From a spiritual standpoint, the Earth possesses the same spirit and consciousness as we do. Every piece of consciousness in the natural world is a portal of purely positive Source Energy. Plants, flowers, trees, rocks, rivers, the sea, and the wind, just like us, have spirit, energy, consciousness, and beingness. A collective term for the spirits and entities of nature is *the elementals*.

The elementals of earth, air, water, fire, and spirit are responsible for the thriving and functioning of our planet. They work individually and collectively to not only preserve our planet's natural functioning, but also to assist humans in flowing and thriving in the same way that nature does. After all, we are also a part of nature.

The elementals want us to stay here. Have you noticed how prominent mermaids, fairies, and unicorns have become in both spiritual and popular culture? These nature spirits are appearing in our consciousness with more regularity because they are actively trying to grab our attention.

They recognize that we've gone astray, notably in our treatment of the environment, and they want to help us get back on track.

The elementals are extending an olive branch so that we can work together and remember how to flow and thrive in harmony with nature in all aspects of our existence, particularly in our relationship to the Earth.

The elementals are divided into five categories:

Earth elementals govern our interactions with the physical world, including with money, our homes, our bodies, and our feelings of safety, security, and protection. They are fantastic at assisting us in manifesting financial prosperity as well as in feeling grounded in our human bodies and lives on this planet. Tree dryads, forest nymphs, mountain giants, and flower fairies are among the various earth elementals known collectively as *gnomes*.

Air elementals are in charge of our thoughts and beliefs, including the ones concerning our past lives. They help us release limiting thoughts and beliefs, allowing for divine guidance to flow freely. They work well with fire elementals to assist us in getting rid of stress and finding serenity. Air elementals, which are collectively known as *sylphs*, include the four winds and various breeze spirits.

Water elementals are in charge of our sexuality, emotions, and relationships. They represent the Divine Feminine and assist us in navigating our emotional landscape. They're relationship experts who can teach us how to appropriately deal with suppressed emotions, how to share vulnerably, and how to create meaningful relationships. Water elementals, which are collectively known as *undines*, include the ocean, lake, and river mermaids, along with water nymphs and sprites.

Fire elementals rule the realms of change, manifestation, motivation, transmutation, and transformation. They represent the Divine Masculine and instill in us the courage to pursue our aspirations and life's purpose. Fire elementals, which are collectively known as

salamanders, include the phoenix, the Earth core and volcano dragons, and various sun dragons.

Spirit elementals oversee our soul path, life's purpose, and career
choices. They are the embodiment of our soul's spirit, bringing forth
our authenticity as well as spiritual wisdom. They understand what
it takes to discover, pursue, and live our life's purpose. They also
collaborate with all other elementals to assist them in channeling
Source Energy through their varied roles. Spirit elementals include
unicorns, pegasians, and the muses.

The elementals' cleansing and shielding abilities are derived from their
unique energy attributes and areas of specialization. You'll learn how to
connect and combine the energies of various elemental spirits to properly
protect your energy in the meditations and processes that follow.

CHAPTER 13

Introduction to Energy Clearing and Shielding

OK—this is the time we've all been waiting for. You now understand the importance of energy protection, you have an in-depth understanding of what energy attack is and how it works, you've met your energy protection guardian, and you've identified the energy attachments currently messing up your vibration. In the following chapters, you'll learn a series of energy clearing techniques, processes, and meditations you can use to free yourself from external attachments and reclaim your energetic authenticity.

Before we dive in, it's important to have the following things in mind:

Remember the Seven Steps of Energy Protection: Before you attempt any of the following processes, it's vital that you first go through the previous steps in the process. I know it is tempting to try things instantly, but trying these processes without first centering, grounding, connecting, and identifying will limit the effectiveness of the processes.

Trust Your Intuition When Choosing Processes: Different clearing processes work for different types of energy attachment. Although I provide some general guidelines as to the types of energy attachments that each process helps clear, it'll be more beneficial for you to use your intuition when choosing processes. Every person is different, and therefore, each type of energy attachment manifests in a different way within your energy field. Whereas one process may work for clearing collective thought forms in my energy field, it may work in a different way for you. Thus, when you're ready to start clearing your energy, consult with your intuition and your energy protection guardian about which processes will be best for you.

Adjust the Processes to Work For You: When it's time to practice the processes, you may feel inspired to adjust them in a way that works in alignment with your spiritual beliefs and spiritual practice. That's totally fine! In my experience, most clearing and shielding processes work best when we make them our own. By personalizing the processes, you're adding your own energy to them, thus strengthening your belief and intention behind their effectiveness.

You'll also find that you already know of, or have practiced, some of the processes that follow. If you already practice them in a specific way that works for you, there's nothing wrong with continuing to do so. You may want to give my rendition of these processes a try to see how you like it, or you can just stick to what has worked for you in the past.

In a few of the processes, I talk about calling upon various spirit guides, gods/goddesses, and elementals. If you don't resonate with any of these deities, or if you'd rather work with another one, trust your guidance and choose one that works best.

Keep An Eye On Your Dependence: I've stressed this many times so far, but I'll keep reminding you because it's absolutely the most important element in energy protection: *you* hold the power to clearing and shielding your energy, not the tools, processes, or spirit guides. All the processes you'll learn work because you intend them to work. Their power draws from your own internal power of protection. The tools and spirit guides you'll connect with aren't external to, but are an extension of, you. The moment you give your power away to, and become dependent on, these processes, you make yourself vulnerable to attack.

OK—you're all set! Let's get started.

CHAPTER 14

Golden Light Net

This is my go-to energy clearing process and the one I use on a daily basis for quick and effective energy clearing. The process simply involves visualizing a golden light net that filters your body and aura, catching and removing energy attachments. It combines the power of intention with the clearing qualities of golden light to clear the milder types of energy attachment, such as collective thought forms and residual spatial energy.

You can also use this process to clear other types of energy attachment, but in most cases, this will require you to combine it with other processes. For example, you could use the golden light net to remove spirit attachments, but in most circumstances, spirits attached to your aura have also managed to create cords of attachment or are stuck there as a result of a karmic contract you have made in a past life. Therefore, for the golden light net process to work in removing complex energy attachments, you may first have to use some of the more advanced processes in this section.

When you clear your energy for the first time, it's best to use this process last because it's great at removing any remaining energy stains and toxic energy from your energy field following the deeper energy clearing work. Once you're done with your first big clearing, you can then use this process as your main clearing tool in your daily energy clearing practice to remove any new, mild types of energy you pick up in your day-to-day affairs.

Here are the steps for practicing the process:

1. Close your eyes, get in a meditative state, and go through the first three steps of the energy protection process—grounding, centering, and connecting.

2. With your 360-degree vision turned on, bring to your mind your energy field with all the energy attachments stuck there.

3. Visualize a wide, tightly squared, etheric net of golden light a few inches below your feet. You may see your energy protection guide, a band of angels, or other spirit guides holding the net and supporting the process.

4. Gradually, visualize the net filter through your body starting from the bottom edge of your aura and moving upward all the way to the upper edge of your energy field above your head. While this happens, you may see the various energy attachments being pulled out of your energy field and being caught in the golden light net.

5. Once you've filtered everything out, tie up the net with your intention and mentally send it to the ethers so that these energy attachments can be transmuted by the beings of light there. You may visualize your protection guide assisting you in this.

6. When you're done, offer gratitude to your guides and come out of the meditation.

You can download an expanded audio recording of this meditation at *GeorgeLizos.com/PYL.*

CHAPTER 15

Dagger Lifting

Dagger lifting is a process exclusively used to deal with psychic attack. It involves using an etheric magnet to remove psychic daggers of attack from your back and subsequently to heal and patch up the energetic wounds to prevent the daggers from reappearing.

As described earlier, psychic attack results from others directing intense feelings of anger and jealousy toward you. These might be people you have a relationship with or complete strangers. In cases where you have a relationship with the other person, the psychic daggers on your back will probably be accompanied by a toxic cord of attachment that you also need to release using the cord-cutting process in Chapter 24. Unless you cut that cord, the dagger can easily reappear the next time that person thinks or feels negatively toward you since your energetic cord gives them direct access to your energy. If you don't have a relationship with the attacker, simply removing the dagger is enough to clear the attack.

It's a good idea to scan your energy for psychic daggers after having an argument with someone, even if you took the time to shield yourself beforehand. Energy shielding isn't foolproof because its protective power is tied to your moment-to-moment vibrational frequency. If your vibrational frequency decreases during the argument, your protective shield weakens, leaving you vulnerable to attack.

I've also had to use this dagger lifting process after being surrounded by a large group of people, such as when I've gone to a shopping center or the movies, when I've been traveling, and so on. On occasions in which I haven't shielded my energy before going out, I've later identified multiple daggers on my back from passersby who happened to have passed judgment, thought negatively of, or gossiped about me. Rather than having the feel of an intense psychic attack, this kind of gossip or mild judgment directed at us results in small, flimsy daggers that don't have a big negative impact on our energy. However, over time, and as these little daggers accumulate, their combined energy can create serious energy blocks and result in the same symptoms as a full-blown psychic attack.

Lastly, it's also important to keep an eye out for any false, self-imposed daggers that may show up on your back, similar to the ones I'd conjure up in my energy field due to my expectation of people attacking or rejecting me (I talked about this in Chapter 9). These are the result of self-sabotaging limiting beliefs and other core issues and can only be fully released when you do the inner work to identify and release them.

Here are the steps for practicing the process:

1. Close your eyes, get in a meditative state, and go through the first three steps of the energy protection process—grounding, centering, and connecting.

2. With your 360-degree vision turned on, scan your back's energy to identify any psychic daggers or other weapons that may be there.

3. As you identify them, spend some time psychically connecting to them and seeing who they're connected to. You may get a mental image of the person, a specific emotion, or a memory of an argument you may have had. Tune in to the energy of each dagger, particularly the ones coming from people you have a relationship with, and notice any toxic cords of attachment related to them.

4. Conjure up a life-size energetic magnet with your mind's eye, and with your intention, turn it on so that it instantly removes

all daggers from your back. Once you've removed everything, let your energy protection guardian send the magnet with the daggers to the ethers so they can be transmuted back into love.

5. To heal and patch up the etheric wounds on your back, visualize emerald green light seeping through them and restoring your energetic field to its most vital state. You may ask Archangel Raphael, Greek god of healing Asclepius, or any other healing deity you work with to assist you with this process.

6. When your back looks shiny and bright again, thank the spirit guides that assisted you and gradually come out of the meditation.

You can download an expanded audio recording of this meditation at *GeorgeLizos.com/PYL.*

CHAPTER 16

Sylph Storm

The *sylphs* are air elementals that channel the energy clearing qualities of air. Doesn't the energy of your house always shift when you open a window and let fresh air in? And, don't you always feel uplifted and energized while you're outside on a particularly windy day? The sylphs are the spirits who drive the wind's dynamic and animating properties and can move energy like no other element. The sylphs are the ones that orchestrate tornadoes and hurricanes year after year, and although these are devastating for humankind, they are unavoidable consequences of the environmental harm we do, and the Earth gladly accepts them.

In the same way that wind moves energy in the physical world it can also move energy in the etheric world. The element of air is associated with our mental functions—our thoughts and belief systems, including past-life beliefs. Since the etheric imprints of our thoughts and beliefs are primarily present within the third mental body of our aura, working with the sylphs and the element of air is most effective when it comes to clearing our aura. You can use the sylph storm process to clear limiting thought forms, residual spatial energy and spirit attachments, and any other energy attachment that lingers in your auric field.

If you get a chance to go out in nature during a particularly windy day, you can also use this process in a more palpable way by mindfully asking the wind sylphs to clear your aura. I often take advantage of wind storms and go out to the beach, a park, or to the mountains, letting the wind work its magic on me. I always feel cleared and uplifted afterward.

Here are the steps to practicing the process:

1. Close your eyes, get in a meditative state, and go through the first three steps of the energy protection process—grounding, centering, connecting.

2. With your 360-degree vision turned on, scan your energy body and aura to identify the various types of energy attachments currently clouding your energy field.

3. As you take long, deep breaths, notice how the element of air manifests in your body. Observe as your chest expands and shrinks with each breath as it welcomes the vital oxygen in the air. Notice how much more peaceful you are as you become mindful of your breathing.

4. Expand your awareness to notice how the element of air manifests in the world around you. Feel the soothing caress of the wind on your face and watch it rustle through the plants, flowers, and trees all around you if you're outside. Recognize how the atmosphere fills the entire planet and serves as a link between all planetary consciousnesses.

5. While connecting to the collective essence of air, mentally or aloud, call upon the collective energy of the air sylphs to manifest. You could say, *I call upon the oversoul of air and the air sylphs to flow through me and rid my aura of all that no longer serves me.*

6. As you say this, you may notice the presence of slender, almost formless air sylphs flying about your body and over your head, or perhaps you'll detect the presence of your air sylph guardian. Take some time to get to know the sylphs and thank them in advance for the clearing.

7. Ask the sylphs to begin circling around the periphery of your aura in a clockwise direction, cleansing negative energy from your aura. They'll fly about you faster and faster, gaining speed and creating a tremendous windstorm or tornado that clears your aura of low-level spirits, thought forms, and other negative energies. Allow the sylphs to work their magic while you take deep breaths.

8. Once the process is complete, take some time to express gratitude to the sylphs for their assistance.

9. When you're ready, end the meditation and drink some water to ground yourself and allow your body's energy to adjust to the shifts.

You can download an expanded audio recording of this meditation at *GeorgeLizos.com/PYL.*

CHAPTER 17

Energy Vacuuming

Energy vacuuming is a powerful process that involves partnering with the cleansing power of the element of air and the sylphs to clear most types of energy attachment. I like to use this technique when I don't have a lot of time on my hands, such as when I'm in a hurry to go somewhere, when I'm staying with friends, or when I'm on vacation. It only takes a few minutes to practice, and it works wonders in clearing your energy.

The process of energy vacuuming involves calling upon the collective oversoul of air and the collective presence of the sylphs or your sylph guide and using an etheric vacuum cleaner to remove energy attachments from your energy body and all auric layers. When I use this technique on myself or with clients, I often like to ask the sylphs to start by placing the mouth of the vacuum cleaner at the top of the crown chakra so that it removes all impurities from the chakra system first; I then proceed by clearing the energy body and finish with the aura.

As mentioned earlier, this process works for most types of energy attack. However, in cases of toxic cords of attachment, psychic daggers, and karmic contracts in which the attack is rooted in past lives or in personal relationships, you may need to combine this process with some of the other processes in this section of the book that work best with these specific energy attachments.

Here are the steps to practicing the process:

1. Close your eyes, get in a meditative state, and go through the first three steps of the energy protection process—grounding, centering, connecting.

2. With your 360-degree vision turned on, scan your energy body and aura to identify the various types of energy attachments currently clouding your energy field.

3. Mentally or out loud, call upon the collective oversoul of air and the air sylphs. You can say something along the lines of *I call upon the collective essence of air and the air sylphs to come into my presence to clear my body and aura of all negative energy.* While doing this, visualize air in all its forms and expressions. Picture breezes, strong winds, and tornadoes, as well as all the ways through which air manifests within you and the world.

4. When you feel the presence of air and the air sylphs with you, visualize the sylphs or your sylph guide holding an etheric vacuum cleaner and placing it at the top of your head. As they turn it on, the tube sucks all energetic impurities out of your chakras, unblocking them and restoring their natural functions. The sylphs then proceed to cleanse the rest of your body, and finally they move to clear your aura, extracting any and all the toxic energy attachments present. Make sure to breathe deeply throughout to support the process.

5. Once the sylphs are done and your energy is cleared, offer your gratitude to the sylphs and come out of the meditation feeling great.

You can download an expanded audio recording of this meditation at *GeorgeLizos.com/PYL.*

CHAPTER 18

Sacred Breath

f there's a process that can truly help you step into your power to protect
your energy, it's undeniably the process of using *sacred breath*. Instead
of using external tools and working with deities, employing sacred breath
asks that you clear energy using your intention and physicality alone.
Although you may conceptually understand that your body is your most
powerful tool for energy protection, it's quite different, and liberating,
when you experience that emotionally and corporally for the first time.
Sacred breath helps you do just that.

Essentially, sacred breathing involves stepping into your energy protection power, and then using your mouth to blow air through your aura
and energy body. With intention and visualization, you let the air expand
through the affected areas in your energy field, blowing away what you
no longer need. Similar to the sylph storm process, with this process you
work with the element of air, but rather than calling upon the air sylphs,
instead you utilize the element and consciousness of air within you.

Although the act of blowing air is quite subtle, your intention and
visualization amplify the air blown, turning it into a potent energy clearing agent. Consequently, you can use sacred breath to clear most types
of energy attachments, especially the ones that usually reside in your

aura, such as collective thought forms, residual spatial energy, and spirit attachments.

Here are the steps to practice the process:

1. Close your eyes, get in a meditative state, and go through the first three steps of the energy protection process—grounding, centering, connecting.

2. With your 360-degree vision turned on, scan your energy body and aura to identify the various types of energy attachments currently clouding your energy field.

3. Proceed by observing how the element of air manifests within your body, particularly via your breathing, and all the ways through which it energizes your body and being.

4. Expand your awareness to see how the element of air manifests around you and in nature. Notice how air manifests in your house and neighborhood, and mentally visualize the various expressions of air in the world—in breezes, wind storms, tornadoes, and hurricanes.

5. Call upon the collective element of air by mentally or verbally saying something along the lines of *I call upon the collective essence of air to come into my presence and clear my body and aura of all negative energy.*

6. Once you've connected with the collective element of air, tighten your lips into a pout and, slowly and ceremonially, start blowing air in the affected areas around your aura and energy body. In areas where you can't physically reach, such as your back or within your body, use your intention to direct the stream of air from your mouth to flow through these areas.

7. When you're done clearing, offer gratitude to the element of air, and yourself, and end the process.

CHAPTER 19

Sacred Smoke

Although working with the elemental spirits of earth, air, fire, water, and spirit is incredibly effective at clearing and protecting our energy, many people prefer to work with the elements in their raw and physical form. This is partly because as physical human beings, we place a higher value on, and have a higher expectation for success with, physical tools and processes, and partly because working with the elements in their natural form engages all our senses and creates a felt sense of protection.

This is particularly true when we work with the combined energy of the elements of fire and air to clear energy using sacred smoke. Smoke has been used in clearing rituals since the dawn of time, and although different cultures have used different herbs, resins, and processes, they have all utilized the affective qualities of smoke to transmute darkness into light.

In this chapter, I'll introduce various ways through which you can work with sacred smoke to clear your personal energy. Although space clearing is outside the scope of this book, you can use the same processes to clear the energy of your house, too.

The Transformative Qualities of Fire and Air

Fire brings change and transformation. It both transcends and embraces form and it creates and destroys energy, so it can both clear and purify people and spaces at the same time. Think of how Earth's tectonic plates interact with each other, forcing one another into the magma and triggering earthquakes and volcanic eruptions that both create and destroy life. Think of how the sun creates all life, but how it can also destroy it if overly consumed. It's no wonder fire has been used, and is still being used, by cultures all around the world to clear and purify people and places, even entire cities and countries.

The element of air is also an agent of change and transformation, but it works on a different level and frequency to transmute energy. Whereas fire destroys and creates form, air simply cleanses and clears the existing form, shifting its energy while allowing it to ascend to its highest potential. Think of what opening a window and letting fresh air into your house does to its energy. It doesn't change its form, but it clears and uplifts it so that it still feels changed and transformed. You also experience this when you're out on a particularly windy day. As you let the wind blow up against your face and body, it clears your vibration and you're left feeling calm and uplifted.

You can work with the energy of fire and air alone to clear your energy, such as with the Candle Cleansing (Chapter 20), Dragon's Breath (Chapter 21), and Sylph Storm (Chapter 16) processes, or you can use the two elements together. When we combine the elements of fire and air to create smoke, and when we strengthen that with the power of our intention, we create *sacred smoke*, which is a powerful tool for clearing energy. The phoenix, one of the most iconic symbols and elementals for transformation, embodies the blended qualities of fire and air and portrays the energetic renewal and transformation that's experienced when we work with these two elements together.

Energy Clearing with Sacred Smoke

Due to its ethereal and otherworldly essence, smoke transforms the profane into the sacred and has thus been used for spiritual purposes since ancient times. Smoke speaks directly to our primordial sense of smell, activating emotions and memories and helping us soften the boundaries between our physicality and spirituality. As a result, smoke can instantly change the energy of people and space, which makes it an excellent agent for energy clearing.

Due to its transmuting qualities, you can use sacred smoke to clear most forms of energetic attachments, including the more complex ones like toxic cords of attachment, karmic contracts, and psychic daggers.

You can use sacred smoke in many ways to clear your energy, but the two most common ones follow.

Using a Smudging Bundle

Smudging involves using a bundle of herbs to produce smoke that you slowly wave around your aura, visualizing it burning away toxic energetic attachments. Although you can use various types of herbs to create a smudging bundle, the two most common herbs are sage and cedar. I personally like to create a blended bundle of sage and rosemary because I find their combined energy particularly effective for clearing intense energy in my aura and house. Working with, and combining, different types of herbs also brings in the nurturing and nourishing qualities of the element of earth and the specific energetic and medicinal qualities of the herbs used.

Although you can easily purchase smudging bundles online or from metaphysical shops, they're always more powerful when you make them yourself and infuse them with your energy and intentions. It's best to gather the herbs at dawn when the energy is clean and fresh; always ask for permission and offer gratitude to the plant while doing so. It's also a good idea to give the plant an offering, usually some fruit, cornmeal, a piece of your own hair, or just your light. It's important to only take a small part of the plant so that it can go on growing and thriving.

When you have your herbs, use a cotton string to tie them tightly together in a stick, and let them dry out. After your smudging bundle has completely dried, you can use it to clear your energy. Place your bundle in a fireproof bowl with an ample amount of sand inside. Light your bundle and then extinguish it to produce smoke. With intention, and after you have gone through the initial steps for energy protection, wave the smoke around your body starting at the top of your head and going all the way down to your feet, visualizing the smoke burning away all energetic attachments. For the attachments within your physical body's energy, use your intention and your hand to channel the energy of the smoke to the affected area.

Burning Loose Herbs and Resin

Burning herbs and resins is my preferred way of working with sacred smoke for energy clearing because it gives me the option of bringing in the energies and medicinal qualities of various other ingredients. Specifically, I like to purchase ready-made herb/resin blends that channel a specific deity, or serve a specific purpose, and use them intuitively to clear different forms of energy attack. For example, if I'm working to release energy attachments around romantic relationships, then I'll work with an Aphrodite herb/resin blend, and when I'm working to clear toxic energy and thought forms having to do with money and career, I'll work with a Pan-inspired blend.

Working with loose herbs and resins in this way allows you to customize the clearing process to target the intricacies of certain energy attachments, which is really helpful when you're dealing with multi-layered energy attachments (i.e., when multiple energy attachments are coming from, and are related to, the same source). That being said, it's not essential that you use a blend of herbs and resins for your energy clearing work; a single herb or resin combined with intention can be enough to perform all clearing. Remember our motto: it is not the tools and processes but *you* that have the power to clear energy.

Before you proceed with burning loose herbs and resin, make sure you have a fireproof bowl filled with enough sand or soil to prevent it from becoming a fire hazard in the off chance the bowl cracks. It's also a good idea to place the bowl on a fireproof surface. You can then place a small charcoal tablet in the bowl and lay your herb/resin blend on it. You can use any herb or resin that you feel attracted to, enjoy the scent of, or wish to work with because of its specific qualities. Some of the most common herbs used are sage, cedar in leaf form, and rosemary, but I also like to use lavender, roses, and olive leaves. When it comes to resins, the most common ones are frankincense, copal, benzoin, and myrrh.

Once you're ready to clear your energy, place the bowl with your selected herbs and resins in front of you, go through the initial energy protection steps, and then use your hands to draw smoke from the bowl around your body. Cupping your palms around the smoke, gently wash your aura starting from the top of your head and moving all the way down to your feet. Similar to smudging, you can direct the energy of the smoke to stuck areas within your physical body with your intention. When you're done, make sure to extinguish the charcoal tablet in a container of water.

CHAPTER 20

Candle Cleansing

andle cleansing is a great technique to use at the end of the day to clear residual spatial energy or other mild energy attachments you may have caught as you went about your day. It works primarily on the first three layers of your aura—the etheric, emotional, and mental bodies—to dissolve negative thoughts and emotions so that you can end the day on a positive note. It's a great process to use if you're suffering from insomnia or light sleep, as by washing away limiting thoughts, emotions, and other energetic stains, you free your body of worry and overwhelm that are often the cause of insomnia.

The process involves working with your hands and the energy of fire and its salamanders (fire elementals found in candles, bonfires, and small-scale expressions of fire) to brush your aura and wash away unwanted energy. All you need to practice it is a candle, your hands, and your intention.

Here are the steps to practicing the process:

1. Close your eyes, get in a meditative state, and go through the first three steps of the energy protection process—grounding, centering, and connecting.

2. With your 360-degree vision turned on, scan the first three layers of your aura to identify any energetic stains or etheric cobwebs

you may have attracted during the day. These could be negative thoughts or emotions or residual energy you may have picked up by interacting with people and spaces.

3. Light your candle, close your eyes, and mentally or verbally call upon the collective presence of fire and the fire salamanders. You can say something along the lines of *I call upon the collective essence of fire and the fire salamanders to come into my presence and clear my aura of negative energy.* While doing this, visualize fire in all its forms and expressions. Picture candles, bonfires, volcanoes, and the sun, as well as all the ways fire manifests within you, the world, and the Universe.

4. Open your eyes and stare into the candle flame, calling upon its salamander spirit to make itself present. You may see, feel, hear, or just know the presence of your candle's salamander as it makes itself present.

5. Once you've established your connection with the collective essence of fire and your candle's salamander, cup your hands around the candle's aura and mentally charge your hands with its energy.

6. Gently and ceremonially brush your palms through your aura in a vertical, downward manner, starting from the top of your head and making your way down to the tips of your toes. Visualize the negative energy imprints you've identified sloughing off of your body and aura with each brush. Replenish the fire energy in your hands as you see fit by cupping your hands around the candle.

7. When you're done, offer gratitude to the salamander guide and then blow out the candle.

CHAPTER 21

Dragon's Breath

There are many types of dragons: elemental dragons within the five elements, dragons residing in other planets, and celestial dragons that exist in the higher dimensions. The elemental dragons of earth, air, fire, water, and spirit are ancient nature beings that have been on the planet since its creation. Fire dragons, specifically, were among the first elementals to live on our planet, and are, to a great extent, responsible for the creation and subsequent evolution of our planet. In its early stages, planet Earth was nothing more than a mass of burning hot gases that wove together to slowly and gradually form the habitable planet we live on today. The fire dragons have been the guiding consciousness behind this cocreative process and still are today in the continuing evolution of the planet.

Given their primordial and indispensable roles in the creation of life, fire dragons fully embody the creative and destructive aspects of fire. As a result, when we partner with them for energy protection, they can help us to both clear and shield our energy. I've often asked my dragon guide Darius to use the same etheric fire to clear all types of energy attachments from my energy, to raise my vibration, and to create a fire shield around my aura that wards off unwanted energy.

You can use the following meditation to work with either the collective essence of the fire dragons or your personal dragon guide to both clear and shield your energy. However, just like the element of fire, the energy of the fire dragons is quite fierce and intense, and although it will clear and shield you against energy attack, it can be quite overwhelming when used excessively. I suggest that you only use this process when you've attracted a great deal of energy attack and need some serious clearing, when you feel you're currently being attacked by someone and need to cast a powerful shield to protect yourself, or when you're feeling low and need an energy boost.

Here are the steps to practicing the process:

1. Close your eyes, get in a meditative state, and go through the first three steps of the energy protection process—grounding, centering, connecting.

2. With your 360-degree vision turned on, scan your energy body and aura to identify the various types of energy attachments currently clouding your energy field.

3. As you take long, deep breaths, observe how the element of fire manifests within your body. Notice your heart beating and the blood flowing through your body, revitalizing you and keeping you warm.

4. Expand your awareness to see how the element of fire manifests around you and in nature. Notice how fire manifests in the electric appliances you use, in candles, in bonfires, and in the warmth of the sun. Mentally observe fire burning in the core of the Earth, in the magma below its surface, and in the lava erupting in volcanoes all around the world.

5. Call upon the collective energy of the fire and the fire dragons by saying something along the lines of *I call upon the collective essence of fire and the fire dragons to come into my presence and clear my body and aura of all negative energy.*

6. As you say this, you may witness fire dragons soaring above your head, or perhaps your dragon guardian will begin coiling around

your body. Take some time to get to know the dragons and express your gratitude for the clearing.

7. Ask the dragons to blow their divine fire through your body with the aim of burning all energy attack that is blocking the natural flow of energy. If you'd like to use the shielding qualities of fire, you may also ask that the fire revitalizes you and raises your vibration, or that it casts a shield of fire around your aura that burns all energy attachments coming toward you.

8. After the process has finished, take some time to offer gratitude to the dragons, thanking them for their service. Then, come out of the meditation and drink some water to ground yourself, allowing your body's energy to adjust to the changes.

You can download an expanded audio recording of this meditation at *GeorgeLizos.com/PYL.*

CHAPTER 22

Sacred Water

Water has been used to cleanse, bless, and purify people and spaces by almost all cultures around the world for thousands of years. The ancient Greeks bathed in rivers and springs before participating in healing rituals and mystery school ceremonies for the purpose of sanctifying their body and energy before making contact with the gods. In the Islamic tradition, people wash their hands and face as a way to cleanse their body and soul before prayer, whereas Christians use baptism to purify and anoint newborn babies and holy water to cleanse and bless their houses. The Indian people consider the Ganges to be a holy river, and many pilgrims bathe in its water daily to clear and purify themselves.

You may also experience the energy cleansing qualities of water within your own spiritual tradition or when you visit various healing wells and holy water springs around the world. Water is also a vital part of taking flower essences and using crystals to cleanse yourself; in baths and showers you use to purify yourself with crystals, salts, and essential oils; or, more simply, when you take a relaxing shower at the end of a busy day. Water has been such a prevalent purifying agent for so many cultures for so long that using it to clear people and spaces has become instinctual knowledge.

In this chapter, I'll delve deeper into the qualities and uses of water for energy clearing and share various ways in which you can utilize it in your own practice.

The Purifying Qualities of Water

Water isn't just a purifying force for humans; it cleanses the entire planet. The oceans' currents work tirelessly to clear and detoxify our planet from the toxins and impurities we've injected it with, in addition to tirelessly transmuting and recycling energy. Inland, rainwater clears the atmosphere of industrial fumes and air pollution and disperses the clouds of toxic energy and collective thought forms that we've emitted into the ether. The delicate balance of the water cycle and its cleansing qualities has been in effect for eons, sustaining the wellbeing of the planet and ensuring its survival.

As a conductor of energy, water has the ability to move and, therefore, transform energy. Whereas fire transforms energy through destruction and creation, water's transformational qualities have to do with the movement and flow of energy. By moving energy, water breaks up stagnancy and rigidity and enables energy to take a different form. From an emotional perspective, water helps us to move, and therefore express, our emotions, shifting them into new and, usually, more positive states, allowing for purification.

Like all elements, the element of water carries spirit, consciousness, and energy. Many spiritual traditions, such as those of the Greeks, Persians, and Indians, have worshipped various water gods, goddesses, deities, and elementals, acknowledging the healing and cleansing properties of different expressions of water. As a result, when we work with water for energy clearing, we don't just benefit from its physical qualities, but we also benefit from the life-force energy, spiritual essence, and elemental spirits within it, which all work in sync to cleanse, bless, and protect us.

Creating Sacred Water

The best way to work with water in a tangible way is to create sacred water, which can then be used in a variety of ways, such as misting, sprinkling, drinking, or adding it to your bath for the purpose of breaking up, clearing, and transforming energy attack.

You can obtain sacred water from shrines and temples within your spiritual tradition; from sacred sources of water such as springs, rivers, wells, the rain, and the ocean; or you can make it yourself. Essentially, sacred water is water that's been instilled with intention, prayer, light, crystals, flowers, and other natural or symbolic elements. When sacred water is obtained from a temple or other holy place, it's infused with the specific intention and prayers of the person or people who created it. When you obtain water from a sacred source, it's instilled with the intention and essence of nature and the elementals that exist in that particular place. When you make it yourself, you get to choose the specific intentions or qualities that you want your sacred water to have.

When I make sacred water for energy clearing and other purposes, I like to take naturally sacred water that I've collected from various sources and charge it with light, crystals, essential oils, flowers, and symbols. For example, I've often used sacred water from the White Spring cave and Chalice Well garden in Glastonbury, UK; Aphrodite's Rock beach in Cyprus; and Castalian Spring at the temple of Delphi in Greece, which I've then combined with other ingredients and intentions in order to make it my own. There really is no right or wrong way to create sacred water as long as you're doing it mindfully and with intention.

If you don't have access to natural water, it's important that you choose water that's been bottled at the source—in a glass bottle—to ensure that it's high vibe and free from plastic contaminants. If you don't have access to this either, you can use tap water that's been left out in the sun for a few hours to help raise its vibration.

Once you have your water, you need to charge it for the purpose of creating sacred water before you use it for energy clearing.

Ways to Charge Water

Water collected from natural sources, temples, and shrines doesn't need to be charged; it's already sacred and you can use it right away to clear your energy using the processes in the following section. However, you may choose to charge it to add your own specific intentions and qualities.

Conversely, tap or bottled water needs to be charged because it has been sitting idle for a while and has probably lost a great deal of its life-force energy and natural energetic imprints. As mentioned earlier, charging water involves using intention, prayers, various sources of light, crystals, flowers, essential oils, and symbols to infuse the water with a certain kind of energy.

The following are the most popular and potent ways to charge water for the purpose of energy clearing.

Celestial Light

The easiest way to charge water is by leaving it out to soak in the light of the sun, moon, and stars. These celestial lights are a reflection of our own inner light and have unique qualities that can help us clear different types of energy attack.

- Sunlight has yang, energizing, and uplifting qualities, and it's great to use when clearing darker energy attachments, such as spirit attachments, psychic daggers of anger or jealousy, and toxic cords of attachment to people, traumatic past lives, and limiting beliefs. Sunlight also has motivating qualities and can be great for clearing the energy of boredom and lethargy, particularly as they relate to following our life's purpose.

- Starlight has yin, feminine, nourishing, and nurturing qualities, and it's great to use when you're feeling exposed and vulnerable, for instance, when you've gone through an argument with someone and are feeling strong waves of negativity coming from them, or when you're feeling overwhelmed after being surrounded by a large group of people. Starlight-infused water will help you to feel safe, nurtured, and protected, while it will also gently peel off the layers of toxic energy you may have attracted.

- Moonlight combines the feminine energy of the moon and the masculine energy of the sun to bring about balance. Moonlight-infused water will help restore balance in your energy field after you've cleared energy attachments, allowing your vibration to naturally rise and strengthen your natural auric defenses. It's a great light to work with as a supplement to other energy clearing practices.

To charge water with celestial light, add it to a glass or ceramic bowl, and then leave it out under your chosen light for at least three hours. It's best to create solar water in the early morning, lunar water during a full moon, and starlight water during the dark phase of the moon.

Prayers and Mantras

The easiest way to create sacred water is by praying over it. In his *New York Times* bestseller *The Hidden Messages in Water*, Japanese scientist Masaru Emoto exposed water to different words, music, and pictures and later froze the water and photographed the resulting crystals. What he discovered was that water exposed to positive thoughts, music, and images created aesthetically beautiful and symmetrical water crystals, whereas water exposed to negative media produced chaotic and disorganized structures. He concluded that water was a "blueprint for our reality," and that our thoughts, words, and energy could alter the physical structure of water.[2]

From this perspective, when we consciously direct our positive intention toward water through prayer and mantras, we literally amplify its structure and instill it with a certain energy. To create sacred water for the purpose of energy clearing, you can use any known prayer or mantra that makes you feel safe and protected, or you can make up your own. Personally, I like to make up my own prayers or spoken intentions, which I then repeat a few times while either holding the bowl of water near my heart or extending my hands out toward it as I visualize my prayers and intentions flowing into it.

Rainbow Water

Charging water with rainbow light is a quick way to energize tap or bottled water, especially when you don't have sufficient exposure to sunlight. Containing all the colors of your chakras, rainbow light both clears and raises the vibration of your chakras and energy body as a whole. Think of the way you feel when you spot a rainbow after a rain storm; your face lights up and your eyes are transfixed by its ethereal beauty. Rainbows reconnect us with our childlike sense of hope, glee, play, and purity—that is, our authentic nature. They remind us that tough situations come and pass, and that eventually, all is well.

To create rainbow water, extend your dominant hand over your glass or bowl of water, and then circle your hand in a clockwise manner while visualizing rainbow light extending outward and into the water. To make it extra potent, you can ask your unicorn guide, or the collective essence of unicorns, to flow the rainbow ray through the water. The *rainbow ray* is a high-vibrational, high-dimensional form of rainbow light that will amplify the potency of your rainbow water (more on the rainbow ray in Chapter 26).

You can use rainbow water alone to clear your energy using the processes in the following section, or you may use it to energize your tap or bottled water before you charge the water further.

Crystal Water

Crystal water is a fabulous way to combine the clearing qualities of earth and water. Stones and crystals all have unique physical and energetic properties, and when used intentionally, they can help us to both clear and shield our energy. Although crystal healing is beyond the scope of this book, you can consult crystal books, websites, or your own intuition to pick crystals holding clearing qualities and use them to create crystal water.

My personal favorite crystals to use for energy clearing purposes are obsidian, black tourmaline, shungite, apophyllite, smoky quartz, amethyst, and rose quartz. To create crystal water, simply place your cleansed crystals in a bowl of water for twenty-four hours to let the water absorb the crystals' energy. It's a good idea to place the bowl of water outside or near a window to let the natural light amplify the charging process.

You may use crystal water for sprinkling, misting, or bathing, but you should never drink it unless you know for certain that it's safe to do so. Whereas certain crystals can be used to create potable drinking water, others include toxic substances such as lead, mercury, and arsenic.

Herb and Flower Water

Another great way of combining the clearing qualities of earth and water is by creating sacred water using flowers, herbs, flower essences, and essential oils. Each flower and plant has unique energetic and medicinal properties, including energy-clearing ones. When you add actual plants and flowers, or their constituents in the form of essential oils and flower essences, to water, you get to create complex and powerful elixirs that you can use for both clearing and protecting your energy.

To create herb or flower water, choose a specific herb or flower and add the actual flowers, flower petals, or leaves to the water. It's best to use natural herbs and flowers that haven't been sprayed to ensure the highest energetic quality. Spend some time connecting to the collective oversoul of your chosen plant by appreciating it for giving you its life force and by asking its spirit to help you clear your energy. Place the bowl of water outside in the morning sun or under the full moon for at least three hours to let the water absorb the vibrational essence of your chosen plant.

If you don't have access to your chosen herb or flower, you can instead add three drops of its essential oil or five drops of its flower essence.

Before you add the drops to the water, spend some time connecting with the collective oversoul of the plant, offering gratitude and asking the plant's spirit for support.

When you go to choose herbs and flowers to work with, you can consult various books, the internet, or your intuition. My personal favorites for energy clearing are lemon verbena, rosemary, sage, pine, cedar, daffodil, and rose.

Always err on the side of caution when it comes to drinking herb and flower water. Whereas some herbs, flowers, and essential oils can be safely consumed, other plants contain toxic substances or pesticides that you may not be aware of. Flower essences can all be safely consumed, however, because they only contain the energetic essence of flowers rather than its physical properties. (Flower essences are different from essential oils. The latter includes chemicals from the flowers, which can be toxic, while the former only includes the flowers' energy.)

Taking Care of Your Sacred Water

After you create your sacred water, it's important to treat it as such. Be sure to use glass or ceramic bottles to store it; avoid plastic containers as they may contaminate the water, both chemically and energetically. If you create different types of sacred water to use for different purposes, you may want to label them. On the label, I like to write both the ingredients of the sacred water and its intended purpose so that I can quickly and easily choose elixirs for different clearing situations as and when I need them. To best preserve your sacred water, keep the bottles in a dark place, such as inside a drawer or cupboard, and at room temperature.

Ways of Using Your Sacred Water

You can use sacred water to clear your energy in several ways. The following are my preferred ways of doing so, but feel free to experiment and use sacred water in a way that makes the most sense to you.

Misting or Spraying

This is my go-to way of using sacred water for energy clearing. *Misting* is primarily used to clear your aura rather than your energy body, and the types of energy attachments that you can clear with it depend on both the energetic qualities of your sacred water and your intention.

To practice this, simply pour your sacred water into a glass spray bottle, or add a few drops of your sacred water to a spray bottle filled with normal water to make it sacred. Before you spray, call upon the collective spirit of water and go through the initial energy-clearing steps discussed in Chapter 7. Then spray generous amounts of water all around your aura, starting from the top of your head and moving all the way down to your feet. Since misting is more suited to clearing your aura, there's no need to spray your body.

Flicking

Flicking is similar to misting, but it's also suited to clearing your physical body's energy as well as your aura's. It involves pouring your sacred water, or a few drops of sacred water, into normal water contained in a glass or ceramic bowl, and then using an herb or flower to flick water on your body and around your aura. I like to use aromatic herbs such as basil, mint, lavender, rosemary, or sage, or any other seasonal herb or flower that feels right at the time. The added benefit of flicking rather than misting is that you can also benefit from the spiritual and energetic medicine of the herbs and flowers you use to flick the water with, which adds an extra layer of clearing to the process.

Drinking

If your sacred water is safe to consume (i.e., it wasn't created using toxic crystals, herbs, or flowers), then there are a few ways you can drink it to clear your energy.

I like to add a few drops of sacred water to a glass of regular water and then drink it mindfully and ceremonially. When doing so, it's important first to take some time before drinking to call upon the collective spirit of water and ask it to flow its presence into your glass of water. Then, take the glass in your hands, bring it up to your mouth, and let the water touch the tips of your lips. Take a small sip, and as you swallow it, visualize the energy of the water expanding through your body and aura, clearing toxic energy attachments. Continue taking sips in a mindful way until you're done.

Another way to drink sacred water for energy clearing is to add it to a glass dropper bottle and take five drops, five times a day. Doing this daily for a month is a great way to not only clear your energy, but also strengthen your natural energetic defenses in the long-term. This is similar to the way you take flower essences and other homeopathic elixirs; it allows the sacred water to go deeper in clearing and strengthening the various layers of your aura and energy body.

Adding It to Your Bath

Taking a cleansing bath by adding different types of salt and essential oils to it is a popular and effective way of clearing your energy. To make your cleansing bath even more potent, you can also add a few drops of your sacred water or simply use the water alone without any additional ingredients. You may even want to turn your bath water into sacred water by using prayer, mantras, crystals, flowers, or rainbow light.

When your cleansing bath is prepared, go through the initial energy-clearing steps and then soak yourself in the water, visualizing all unwanted energy attachments flushing out of your body and into the bathwater. I've found cleansing baths to be more effective than misting, flicking, or drinking water, simply because they allow you to immerse yourself in a body of water for a longer period of time, allowing for a deeper cleansing.

An alternate, more natural way to have a cleansing bath is by bathing in the sea, a lake, a river, or a waterfall. As I mentioned at the beginning of this chapter, natural water is already sacred because it holds the energetic imprints of the Earth, sun, moon and stars, as well as the collective energy of the elemental kingdom.

Water is a powerful transmuter of energy, and these are just a few of the ways that you can use it for energy clearing. Use these processes as they are, or let them inspire you to find new ways of using water to cleanse and purify your energy field.

CHAPTER 23

Unicorn Shower

I first read about unicorn showers in Diana Cooper's book *The Wonder of Unicorns*, and I've since evolved the process to match my own understanding of energy clearing and unicorns. Unicorns are spirit elementals and spiritual extensions of our souls that facilitate the exchange of divine intelligence and life-force energy between our physical and spiritual presence.

Unicorns embody our authentic nature and, thus, hold the blueprint to finding and following our life's purpose. Each one of us has a unicorn spirit guide who stands as the embodiment of our authentic self, in tune with our life's purpose and holding the knowledge of how we can follow and fulfill it. In my second book, *Lightworkers Gotta Work*, I included several guided unicorn meditations focused on finding and following our life's purpose. In this book, I'll focus on unicorns' ability to help us align with our true essence and nature—our energetic authenticity.

Taking a unicorn shower involves asking your unicorn guide to infuse your bath or shower water with the rainbow ray, which both clears and uplifts your energy. The *rainbow ray* is a high-vibrational, high-dimensional divine light that holds the highest frequency of all the colors of the rainbow, and it can raise the vibration of anything it comes into contact with. The unicorns channel the rainbow ray on a human level so that we can work with it to amplify our energy.

Turning your evening shower into a unicorn shower is a great way to clear your energy and uplift your vibration at the end of the day. This process combines the cleansing and purifying qualities of water with the uplifting energy of the rainbow ray to clear most of the energy attachments you attract during your day, such as residual spatial energy, thought forms, and minor cases of psychic attack.

Here are the steps to practicing the process:

1. Close your eyes, get in a meditative state, and go through the first three steps of the energy protection process—grounding, centering, connecting.

2. With your 360-degree vision turned on, scan your energy body and aura to identify the various types of energy attachments currently clouding your energy field.

3. Your heart is the doorway of your soul and the element of spirit within you. Placing your hands on your chest, visualize a tiny dot of white light in the center of your heart, representing your soul's energy coming through. With each breath you take, visualize this white dot of light growing bigger and bigger, until it expands to fill up your entire body and aura. This light is the energy of soul that animates your being and consciousness; it acts as a bridge between your physical and spiritual perspectives.

4. Expand your awareness to notice how the element of spirit manifests in the world around you. Observe how all animate and inanimate beings and objects have divine intelligence flowing through them at all times, how our planet moves in space in perfect proximity to other planets, and how life and the Universe all work according to this divine intelligence.

5. As you connect to the collective essence of the element of spirit, mentally or out loud, call upon your unicorn guide to make itself present. You could say, *I call upon my unicorn guide to come into my presence and clear my body and aura of all that no longer serves me.*

6. At this moment, you'll either see, feel, hear, or just know your unicorn guide is making itself present. Ask your unicorn to point its horn, also known as the alicorn, toward the water flowing from the shower head and infuse it with the rainbow ray with the purpose of clearing all unwanted energy attachments and raising your vibration.

7. Proceed by stepping under the water and letting it flow over you. Visualize the energy of the rainbow-infused water flowing through your physical body and expanding through your aura, dissolving anything you've absorbed during the day that isn't aligned with your authentic self.

8. When you feel you've cleared yourself fully, both physically and energetically, offer your gratitude to your unicorn guide and come out of the shower feeling uplifted.

CHAPTER 24

Cutting Toxic Cords
of Attachment

You can utilize numerous tools, methods, and spirit guides to cut toxic cords of attachment, just as you can use several ways to clear your etheric body, aura, and chakras. However, my preferred method of cutting attachment cords does not require any instruments or spiritual beings; instead it relies solely on our physical bodies, particularly our hands.

As I previously stated, the only tools you actually need for spiritual clearing and protection are your body and intention; all other instruments and spiritual beings are only there to help amplify and reinforce your own power. Despite the fact that we might readily cut cords of attachment with such tools and beings, I believe it is more effective to keep this a totally personal task, given the intimate character of these cords.

Toxic cords of attachment, unlike other types of energy attachments—such as collective thought forms, low-level spirits, and residual spatial energy, which you often pick up spontaneously and unconsciously as you go about your daily life and interact with people and spaces—are created deliberately over time. The majority of these ties are formed as a result of the time and energy you spend deliberately with others—moments shared and words exchanged. Although these cords may have been positive at the start of a relationship, they have since become negative as the relationship has deteriorated.

The same may be said for your toxic cords of attachment to places, objects, beliefs, deceased pets, past lifetimes, and so on. Even though these aren't living beings, you can still interact with their energy and beingness. In the same way that you have relationships with people, you have relationships with these places, limiting beliefs, objects, and past lives.

Because of the intimacy of these relationships, I've discovered that properly releasing them requires an equally intimate process, and our physicality is the ideal tool for this.

The Cord-Cutting Process

Follow these steps to cut and release the toxic cords of attachment you have to the people, places, objects, beliefs, and past lives that you've identified in your scanning session:

1. Close your eyes, get in a meditative state, and go through the first three steps of the energy protection process—grounding, centering, connecting.

2. Scan your energy body and aura with your 360-degree vision turned on to identify the various toxic cords of attachment that are currently clouding your energy field.

3. Spend some time carefully touching each cord and following it to discover where it leads. You'll get a feel for the person, location, object, belief, or past life it's linked to as you interact with it. During this process, be careful not to stir up any anger, hurt, or resentment, as this will only strengthen your attachment. Simply look at the cords and make mental notes of what they mean.

4. Now that you've discovered all of the cords, it's time to cut them and let go of these relationships. Come into your power to clear energy while sitting or standing, with your eyes open or closed.

Feel the life-force energy flowing through you, linking you to the heavens above and the ground below, and know and affirm that you have all you need to let go of these toxic connections completely.

5. Consider your dominant hand as a useful tool in this process. When you're ready, spread your fingers so that your palm is wide and extended, and quickly run your hand through each cord, cutting each using your hand as an energetic knife. While you're doing this, say silently or aloud, *I entirely and completely release you from my life.* Send love and thanks to the people, places, objects, beliefs, and past lives who have taught you so much. Negative, angry, or resentful energy will hinder the cord cutting, so avoid it. Between each cut, take a few deep breaths to refocus your energy.

6. After you've severed all the cords, sit quietly for at least five minutes to allow your body to acclimate to the new changes while you send love and thanks to what you've released.

7. When you feel like the process is finished, end the meditation and take a shower to clear and ground your energy.

You can download an expanded audio recording of this meditation at *GeorgeLizos.com/PYL.*

Dealing with Sticky Cords

When it comes to cutting cords of attachment, it's important to remember that the job isn't finished once the cord is cut. When cutting the cord, you energetically release that person, place, object, belief, or past life, setting the intention that you no longer wish to be negatively affected by it. That being said, your physical bond with that entity may still exist. You might still see these people on a daily basis, have negative beliefs, or hang out in certain places. As a result, some of these cords may reappear, reestablishing your toxic attachments.

To avoid this, you must be prepared to do the real-life work that will emerge shortly after the cord-cutting session. After you've released these attachments spiritually, and so changed your own energy, you'll attract situations, encounters, and circumstances that will allow you to release them physically as well.

For instance, you might have the opportunity to have a heart-to-heart with some of these people in which you calmly but assertively end or transition your relationship with them. You might get a job offer in a different city, or you might feel compelled to make a change in your life that includes letting go of an object or substance. You might feel inclined to read a book, attend a workshop, or enroll in an online course that contains all of the information you require to totally transcend a limiting belief or heal a past-life trauma.

It's critical that you seize these opportunities when they present themselves. Your ego will almost certainly intervene, attempting to hinder the healing process by appeasing these people, by suppressing your pain, and by keeping you in denial about what you've gone through. This is the time to be aware of such sabotaging thoughts and to muster the courage to ignore them and complete the cord-cutting process.

PART III

Shield Your Energy

CHAPTER 25

Introduction to Energy Shielding

Now that you have identified and cleared toxic energy attachments from your energy field, you're ready to shield yourself using various layers of light. These shields will act as your energetic armor as you go about your day, keeping your vibration high, strengthening your energetic defenses, and repelling energy attack.

If you've practiced energy shielding before, chances are you'll be familiar with shielding yourself with white light, or with asking Archangel Michael to surround you with purple light. You might have also used crystals such as black tourmaline and obsidian to ward off unwanted energy, or you might have asked your guardian angels to act as your spiritual bodyguards when you knew you'd be around energy vampires. Although these are all excellent ways of shielding your energy, they don't all work for every type of energy attack. In the same way we wear different clothes for different occasions, we also need to use different protective shields, or a combination of shields, when we expose ourselves to different people, places, and circumstances.

In this part of the book, I'll introduce a more sophisticated way of shielding your energy; one that helps you to choose and combine the right energy shields for each situation.

Types of Shields

There are three types of shields you can use when it comes to protecting your energy from energy attacks:

Repelling Shields: Just as the name suggests, the aim of these shields is to repel negative energy. Rather than simply strengthening your natural protection mechanism, repelling shields add an additional protective layer to your aura that wards off incoming energy attachments.

As a result, repelling shields are useful to cast if you're out and about and exposed to unfamiliar people or places, such as when you go out to bars, restaurants, concert halls, and other public areas. They're also excellent for protecting yourself from toxic people, especially during arguments, and they work well during interactions with toxic family members and energy vampires.

Repelling shields come in various levels of strength, ranging from gentle, to strong, to impenetrable. Often, the strength of the shield depends on the way you program it, whereas at other times, it has to do with the specific characteristics of a particular shield. Gentle repelling shields are commonly used as daily shields to protect against energy fluctuations in your surrounding environment, while stronger and impenetrable repelling shields are used in situations in which you're exposed to a great deal of negativity.

When casting impenetrable repelling shields, it's important to be mindful, as they can often block you from having meaningful social interactions (shielding with an impenetrable shield can sometimes feel like dissociation). Your aura shrinks to allow the shield to completely surround you, causing you to detach your thoughts and emotions from what's going on around you. This keeps you energetically safe until you've removed yourself from the situation.

For this reason, it's best to only use impenetrable repelling shields when you consciously know you're under energy attack or are about to enter a particularly toxic environment. I've personally used impenetrable shields when attending hospitals and funerals or when I've been feeling emotionally attacked or bullied.

Amplifying Shields: Rather than repelling toxic energy, these shields strengthen your natural energy defenses by raising your vibration. They're like spiritual vitamins that seep through your aura and energy body, strengthening their vibration so that you're not so easily affected by external negativity. The higher your vibrational frequency, the lower the chances are that you'll pick up energy attachments, and the more adept your energy field will be at repelling incoming energy attachments that come your way.

What I like about amplifying shields is that they don't cut you off from the world in the same way that repelling shields do; thus they allow you to interact and be sociable with people while still maintaining strong energetic boundaries. For this reason, they're great shields to use when interacting with familiar people and places, such as when you're hanging out with friends, colleagues, and family in your daily affairs.

Transmuting Shields: These are powerful shields that neither repel negative energy nor amplify your own energetic defenses; instead, they transform incoming energy attachments into purely positive energy. Rather than shielding you from the shadow aspects of life, transmuting shields help you to embrace the darkness and show you how to transform it into light.

Transmuting shields are excellent for people working in care industries, such as doctors, nurses, therapists, healers, intuitives, or anyone who has frequent interactions with people. They allow you to be present and empathetic without taking on other people's pain or absorbing their negative energy.

Although categorizing shields is useful when it comes to choosing what shields to use in various situations, it's important not to let these categorizations limit you. The most important element of a shield's protective power is the intention behind it, and the categorizations I share are based largely on my own personal experiences, as well as my observations of other people's experiences. We all have different perceptions of energy, so it's important to not let my or anyone else's experience limit yours.

Layering Your Shields

Depending on the situation you're in, you may want to use a combination of shields. Here are some basic guidelines to help you get started with layering shields:

- **Start with an amplifying shield and add more shields as required.** This is the foundational way to layer your shields. Since amplifying shields strengthen your natural auric defenses, they're great to use on a daily basis. Depending on the people and places you'll be exposed to on any given occasion, you may then add an extra repelling or transmuting shield to complement the energies.

- **Layer repelling and transmuting shields mindfully.** Repelling shields ward off energy, while transmuting shields receive and transform it. As a result, although layering them wouldn't necessarily interfere with their functionality, these shields are not the most ideal match. That being said, you could program a repelling shield to ward off a specific kind of energy, while at the same time programming a transmuting shield to transform a different kind of energy; this would allow you to layer them effectively.

- **Don't layer shields of the same category.** Using multiple repelling or transmuting shields may make you feel detached and out of place. Repelling shields are defensive in nature and have the ability to close you off from the rest of the world, so using more than one at any given time may prevent you from having meaningful interactions with people. When it comes to transmuting shields, using more than one at the same time may hinder their transmuting abilities, leaving you exposed to toxic energy. Each transmuting shield works in complex, alchemical ways to transform energy. A second transmuting shield may interfere with, or block, the transmutation process of the first one.

Layering various different amplifying shields can also have drawbacks; notably making you feel lightheaded and spaced out. Due to their intense, high-vibe qualities, when layered, several amplifying shields can uncenter and unground you, preventing you from having meaningful interactions with people and being fully present in the physical space you're in.

Furthermore, layering shields of the same category implies that you don't trust the initial shield to protect you sufficiently. Your doubt weakens both the initial shield and the combined powers of the additional shields.

- **Layer a maximum of three shields.** Although it can be tempting to shield yourself with as many shields as possible, it's best to cap it at three.

There are a few reasons for this:

- First, shielding yourself with multiple shields can be a sign of codependency and giving away your power. As I've repeated several times throughout this book, *you* hold the power to protect yourself; all energy protection processes do is help you channel that power. Frantically shielding yourself with many layers indicates insecurity in your protective power, as well as overdependence on external factors.

- Second, the more shields you use, the more barriers you create between yourself and the outside world. Although it's important to protect yourself, overdoing it will only lead to isolation and detachment from humanity and life in general. It's important to remember that we're social creatures who need human interaction to thrive and find fulfilment in life, and so rather than hide under multiple shields, give yourself permission to have some contrasting experiences by interacting with the shadow aspects of people and life, learning the lessons that present themselves as a result.

- Lastly, as I explained earlier, layering multiple contrasting shields may lead to them inhibiting one another's functions, thus leaving you vulnerable and unprotected.

As a rule of thumb, the basic formula for layering your shields starts with being clear about the kind of protection you need in any given circumstance. It's always a good idea to start with an amplifying shield to strengthen your energy field before you add a combination of repelling and transmuting shields to respond to whatever energy you're being exposed to.

CHAPTER 26

Rainbow Light Shield

The *rainbow ray*, or simply *rainbow light*, is a high-vibrational energy brought forth by ascended beings of the element of spirit, such as unicorns. You have access to the collective essence of the unicorn realm, which are spirit elementals, in addition to your unicorn guide, who is a spiritual extension of your soul.

Made up of all the colors of your chakras in their purest and highest vibrating frequency of light, the rainbow ray has the power to raise your vibration and strengthen your natural energy defenses to the point where you can't be energetically attacked. When you're living from the perspective of your ego, energy attack only affects you if your vibration is a match for it. When you elevate your frequency by soaking in rainbow light, you become impervious to all forms of energy attack and negativity.

While teaching my online course Unicorn Bootcamp, I first met the rainbow ray after connecting with my unicorn guide, Xeros. Xeros and the unicorn realm's combined presence guided me to let my unicorn's horn, the alicorn, touch each one of my chakras. They explained that the alicorn, instead of being a physical horn, was a high-vibrating light capable of recalibrating any piece of consciousness it came in contact with. I felt a burst of energy flowing through my body when Xeros's alicorn touched my chakras, and I instantly felt connected to Source.

This seemingly white light was actually the rainbow ray, which I didn't realize at the time. Apart from the fact that the rainbow's seven colors combine to form white light, the colors inside the rainbow ray are so highly vibrational that even when you experience them individually, their energy is so strong that all you see is white light. I've been working consciously with Xeros, the unicorns, and the rainbow ray to bathe in this light every day since then.

Follow these steps to shield yourself with rainbow light:

1. Enter a meditative state and call upon your unicorn guide.

2. Once your unicorn has made its presence known, pay attention to its horn, the alicorn. Consider how brilliant it is and how powerful it is in recalibrating anything it comes into contact with.

3. Ask that your unicorn use the tip of its horn to touch your third eye chakra. The rainbow ray will enter your third eye chakra through the horn and then spread throughout your entire body and aura. You may notice a shift in your energy as soon as this occurs.

4. Allow your unicorn to transmit the rainbow ray for a few minutes, or until you notice a considerable increase in your vibration. Thank your unicorn and ask them to end the transmission when you feel you've received enough light.

5. Meditate in this state for a while. Ask the rainbow light to stay with you for as long as you need it today so that you only attract experiences that match its high vibration.

6. When you're ready, come out of the meditation feeling energized and elated and go about your day.

You can download an expanded audio recording of this meditation at *GeorgeLizos.com/PYL*.

CHAPTER 27

White Light Bubble

Shielding yourself with white light is by far the most popular energy shielding technique. In my journey of learning about energy and the spirit world via self-help books, events, courses, and online programs, the instructors always suggested that we shield ourselves with white light as a means of protecting our energy. In time, and as I deepened my understanding of energy, I eventually realized that although white light shielding is indeed a powerful protection technique, it's not a one-size-fits-all process. White light shielding works, but only for specific purposes as is true with all other shielding processes.

We're made out of love and light. I'm sure you've heard this phrase thrown around casually in spiritual communities. What this means is that the essence of who we are, our soul, which is an extension of Source, is loving in nature. Furthermore, our physicality is quite literally made up of light. Quantum physics suggests that when you zoom into every single physical piece of consciousness, including your physical body, what you find is vibration, which also expresses as light.

In essence, when you shield yourself with white light, you shield yourself with the love and light that you're made of. The reason this process has become so popular is because it prompts you to connect with your essence and inner being, the truth of who you are. When you're in full alignment with the love and light that you are, you're safe and protected against anything that's not a match to it. Therefore, shielding yourself with white light amplifies your natural energetic defenses and raises your vibration, limiting your ability to attract negative energy attachments.

However, white light doesn't repel or transmute negative energy, in my experience. Therefore, when its potency wears off and your vibrational frequency oscillates, you become vulnerable to energy attachments that match your newfound lower vibration. The mistake many people make with white light shielding is that they expect it to repel and transmute negative energy rather than recognizing that its protective abilities have a limit.

White light is similar to rainbow light, in that it consists of all the colors of the rainbow. Although both processes have strong amplifying qualities and help you align with the essence of your inner being, they express that in different ways. White light applies a single vibrational frequency to every single piece of consciousness within your body and being, whereas rainbow light functions in a focused way to apply a unique vibrational frequency to each of the seven chakras and auric layers. Due to its focused approach, I consider rainbow light shielding to be stronger than white light in amplifying our energetic defenses.

Use the following steps to shield your aura using white light:

1. Close your eyes and come into a meditative state.

2. Breathing deeply, focus on your heart chakra in the center of your chest. Your heart chakra is the doorway to your soul, bridging your physical and spiritual bodies. Within your heart chakra there's a tiny ball of white light, representing your soul and true essence.

3. With each breath, visualize the tiny dot of light growing bigger, expanding through your chest, your body, and outward to envelop your aura. As it grows larger, it saturates every piece of consciousness within your body, recalibrating and raising its frequency.

4. Set your intention that the white light stays within and around you throughout the day, or for as long as you need it to, keeping your vibration high so that you only attract loving, joyful energy.

5. When you feel complete, come out of the meditation feeling uplifted and high vibe.

You can download an expanded audio recording of this meditation at *GeorgeLizos.com/PYL.*

CHAPTER 28

The Mirror Shield

Mirror shields are powerful, impenetrable repelling shields that you can use to protect yourself against intensely negative people. The process of casting a mirror shield involves visualizing a mirror between you and another person, or visualizing a mirror globe all around your body that repels incoming toxic energy. Often, people advise against using mirror shields because they reflect the toxic energy back to the person who sent it, thus energetically harming them. The way I see it, the person sending this toxic energy already suffers from it, so receiving it back won't do any more harm than they've already done to themselves.

I often see people using mirror shields on a daily basis as their main protection shield. Although using this shield daily will make you impervious to incoming energy attachments, it may also prevent you from authentically and empathically engaging with people. Due to mirror shields' reflective and defensive nature, using them excessively may influence your outlook on people and the world, making you guarded and aloof.

Wearing a mirror shield on a daily basis is akin to always wearing a raincoat, just in case you get caught in a storm. It's unnecessary, restrictive, and uncomfortable. What you'd rather do is have the raincoat on hand for when you need it. Similarly, you'd want to have your mirror shield in your spiritual toolkit and only wear it in situations in which you find yourself in an energetic storm of toxic people and circumstances. For example, I often use mirror shields when I'm caught up in a negative or confrontational interaction with someone, when I notice angry drivers around me while in my car, or any time I feel that someone is consciously sending negative energy toward me.

You can use the following process to cast a mirror shield while you're physically present with someone who's sending negative energy toward you or while you're in your meditation space and want to ward off a consistent energy attack coming from a particular person or group of people who aren't physically present.

Use the following process to cast a mirror shield:

1. With your mind's eye, briefly scan your energy as well as the other person's energy to see how they may be sending toxic energy your way. You will likely see this as energetic daggers shooting out of their aura and directed toward you.

2. Depending on where the other person is positioned in relation to you, visualize a powerful etheric mirror between you, with the reflective side facing the other person. Having done this, notice how the mirror reflects the toxic energy back to its source. Mentally program the mirror to shift around your aura as you or the other person moves around the space, ensuring that it effectively repels the incoming attack. If you're surrounded by multiple toxic people, you can visualize a globe mirror surrounding your aura, reflecting all negative energy outward and back to its source.

3. Leave the mirror shield in place for as long as you're in the presence of the toxic people or situation, and be sure to take it down as soon as you've left.

You can download an expanded audio recording of this meditation at *GeorgeLizos.com/PYL.*

CHAPTER 29

Elemental Shields

Aside from working with the energy clearing and shielding power of nature by connecting with nature beings such as fairies, dragons, sylphs, and mermaids, we can also work with the collective energy of the elements. Due to their dynamic qualities, the elements can be used to both clear and shield us from toxic energy attachments. In this chapter, we'll focus on the shielding qualities of the elements, but feel free to adjust the processes and use them to clear your energy, too.

Unlike most static shields, such as the mirror, white bubble, and rainbow light shields, elemental shields emulate the dynamism of nature and so they're constantly active, moving, and changing. This both adds to, and preserves, their protective qualities, and so elemental shields tend to last longer than other shields. I once shielded my entire flat with the element of earth, by visualizing my house transforming into a forest full of magical earth elementals such as elves, gnomes, nymphs, and fairies. I set it up and let it go, forgetting completely about it. A few weeks later, I noticed a potted plant I'd thought died a long time ago spontaneously burst to life. Tuning in to the energy of the plant, I'd realized that the earth shield I'd set up was very much still in action, and the elemental beings I'd invited in had tended to and resurrected my plant!

In this chapter, I'll introduce the shielding qualities of the elements of earth, air, fire, and water, and guide you through processes you can use to shield yourself (and your house, if you wish).

Earth Shields

There are many ways to shield yourself with the energies and qualities of the Earth, but I'll share with you my favorite five shields, to guarantee maximum protection. These are the mountain, forest, wind, fire, and water shields.

Mountain Shield

Casting a mountain shield involves exactly what the name suggests. By calling upon the collective essence of the earth, and the collective spirit of the mountain giants—the spirits, consciousness, and animism of mountains—you leverage their ancient protective qualities. Mountains have been on our planet for thousands of years, protecting humans and animals alike from invaders and extreme weather conditions. They stand tall and proud despite external adversity, giving us the strength to do the same in our own lives. Mountains have been through so much; they've seen a lot, and they're still standing, reminding us that no matter what may be going on in the world and in our lives, all will eventually be well.

When we cast a mountain shield around our aura, we remind ourselves of our own resilience and tenacity, while simultaneously creating an impenetrable protective shield that repels all incoming negative energy.

Follow these steps to cast a mountain shield:

1. Closing your eyes, come into a meditative state. As you take long, deep breaths, notice how the element of earth manifests in your body. Become aware of the texture, weight, and presence of your body in the environment you're in.

2. Expand your awareness to notice how the element of earth manifests in the world around you. Take note of the dirt beneath your

feet, as well as the plants, trees, and flowers that call it home. Beyond that, look for the element of earth in all living things around you, both live and inanimate. Recognize that the earth element is the source of all physicality.

3. Mentally or out loud, call upon the collective energy of earth and the mountain giants to make themselves present. You could say, *I call upon the oversoul of earth and the mountain giants to make themselves present.* As you say this, you may notice the presence of the mountain giants around you. They'll appear in any way that makes sense to you. Take some time to make your acquaintance with them, and then thank them in advance for the shielding.

4. To cast the shield, visualize your aura surrounded by a tall, thick, and impenetrable mountain range. Everywhere you look, you're surrounded by mountains that act as your personal energetic bodyguards, repelling all sorts of negative energy and people coming your way. Ask the mountain giants to uphold the shield for as long as you need it, and stay in this position for as long as you want to feel safe and protected.

5. When you're done, offer your gratitude to the mountain giants and come out of the meditation.

Forest Shield

Unlike the repelling qualities of a mountain shield, a forest shield around you or your house brings in the refreshing, uplifting, amplifying qualities of forests. Remember the last time you were out in the woods? How did you feel? When I go out in a forest, I feel like I enter a new world. Away from the hustle and bustle of daily life, I let myself become part of a different kind of society—that of nature and all her inhabitants. I make friends with the trees, walk barefoot on the wet grass, collect herbs and wildflowers, listen to the carefree songs of birds and other critters. I quickly feel aligned, connected, and completely over any issue I've been struggling with. The collective aura of forests is so overwhelmingly loving and joyful from all the different plants and creatures that encompass it, that it swiftly and effectively clears and uplifts my aura.

Casting a forest shield re-creates the uplifting and amplifying qualities of forests around you, both clearing and amplifying your energy field. What's special about forest shields that's different from other elemental shields is that with forest shields, you benefit from the protective qualities of all the elementals in a forest, rather than a specific type of elemental. These are usually earth elementals such as elves, gnomes, tree dryads, forest nymphs, and fairies.

Follow these steps to cast a forest shield:

1. Closing your eyes, come into a meditative state. As you take long, deep breaths, notice how the element of earth manifests in your body. Become aware of your body's texture, its weight, and the way it is present in the space you're in.

2. Expand your awareness to notice how the element of earth man- ifests in the world around you. Notice the earth beneath you, along with the plants, trees, and flowers that inhabit it. Beyond that, observe the element of earth in all physical life around you, including both animate and inanimate objects. Realize that all physicality is an extension of the earth element.

3. Mentally or out loud, call upon the collective energy of Earth and the earth elementals to make themselves present. You could say, *I call upon the oversoul of Earth and the earth elementals to make themselves present.* As you do this, visualize a dense forest with all kinds of trees, plants, and elementals. This could be a specific forest you have a connection with, or any forest that comes to mind.

4. As you say this, you may notice the presence of the different earth elementals around you. These could be elves, gnomes, tree dryads, forest nymphs, and fairies, among others. They'll appear in any way that makes sense to you. Take some time to make

your acquaintance with them, and then thank them in advance for the shielding.

5. To cast the shield, visualize yourself sitting or standing in the forest you've chosen. Feel the trees and plants recalibrating your aura and the various earth elementals both clearing and amplifying your energy field. As you visualize this, you'll feel your vibration rising and thus feeling more loving and joyful, mirroring the dominant vibrational frequency of the forest. Set the intention that the energy of the forest stays with you for as long as you need it.

6. When you're done, offer your gratitude to the forest and its elementals and come out of the meditation.

Wind Shield

Although immaterial, wind carries immense energy that can create and destroy worlds. It erodes and shapes the land, powers the ocean's currents, and regulates the earth's atmosphere through jet streams, tornadoes, hurricanes, and other wind phenomena. I most potently experienced the power of the wind when I visited and drove in Iceland in 2014. The complex interaction between the ocean, glaciers, and volcanoes creates powerful winds that can literally throw you off course. On many occasions during my stay there, the wind was so strong that I had to fight to keep the car on the road.

It is this fierce and dynamic energy that we want to leverage when we cast a protective wind shield. In Chapter 16 you learned how to create a sylph storm for the purpose of clearing energy attachments from your energy field; you can use that same process to protect yourself against energy attack. It all has to do with intention and programming. That being said, since wind can express in many forms and shapes, you can create wind shields of various degrees of protection depending on your needs. Although wind can both repel and transmute energy, I personally prefer to use it solely for its repelling properties and use a fire shield for transmutation. In my experience, although wind moves energy, it doesn't transmute it fully into something positive; rather it displaces it. On the other hand, fire completely burns and re-creates energy.

Follow these steps to cast a wind shield:

1. Closing your eyes, come into a meditative state. As you take long, deep breaths, notice how the element of air manifests in your body. Observe as your chest expands and shrinks with each breath as it welcomes the vital oxygen in the air. Notice how much more peaceful you are as you become mindful of your breathing.

2. Expand your awareness to notice how the element of air manifests in the world around you. If you're outside, feel the gentle caress of the wind on your face and see it gently rustling through the plants, flowers, and trees. Become aware of how the atmosphere fills up the entire planet, acting as the connecting link between all planetary consciousnesses.

3. Mentally or out loud, call upon the collective energy of air and the air sylphs to make themselves present. You can say, *I call upon the oversoul of air and the air sylphs to flow through me and shield my aura from all that no longer serves me.* As you say this, you may notice the presence of slender, almost formless air sylphs flying playfully above your head and around your body or even the presence of your sylph guardian from the element of air. Take some time to make your acquaintance with the sylphs and thank them in advance for the clearing.

4. Ask the sylphs to start circling through and around the periphery of your aura in a clockwise manner, creating a tornado of varying strength depending on the protection you need. Feel the wind gathering momentum and use the actual wind you may be surrounded with to strengthen and add to your shield. Set your

intention that the wind shield stays with you for as long as you need it to repel all incoming hostile energy.

5. After the process has finished, take some time to offer gratitude to the sylphs, and when you're ready, come out of the meditation.

Fire Shield

Fire both creates and destroys, making it a powerful shield that transmutes negative energy to love and light. Fire has been one of the primal elements in the creation of our planet, and is, therefore, the basis of all life. At the beginning, the Earth was nothing more than a mass of fiery gas that eventually and gradually evolved into the planet we know today.

To this day, we can see fire at its most primal state when we observe the way plate tectonics work. As a tectonic plate gets subducted into the magma in one part of the world, the subsequent pressure results in a volcanic eruption in a different part of the world, creating new land. The same cyclical process of destruction and creation is emulated in the various expressions of fire, including in our own bodies. For example, our digestive system breaks down the food in our stomach only to transform it into energy that we'll then use to create another cycle of destruction and creation.

We can leverage the contrasting qualities of fire to both clear and shield ourselves. In Chapter 21, you learned how to clear and recalibrate your body and energy by working with the dragons' etheric fire. In this section, you'll learn how to cast a fire shield around your aura with the purpose of transmuting incoming negative energy.

I usually use this shield when I know I'm about to hang out with a toxic group of people or enter a particularly overwhelming or negative space, such as when I go to funerals and visit hospitals and cemeteries. I also like to use it when I'm surrounded by large groups of people, such as when I'm in shopping centers, at movie theaters, or at concert venues, to protect myself from feeling overwhelmed by the energy surrounding me. The fire shield ensures that any incoming negative energy is instantly transformed into love and light, making me immune to external negativity for the duration that I keep it on. In addition to shielding myself with fire, I also ask the fire dragons to clear any space I'm about to enter with their etheric fire, in advance, raising the vibration of the space for others and myself.

Follow these steps to cast a fire shield:

1. Closing your eyes, come into a meditative state. As you take long, deep breaths, notice how the element of fire manifests in your body. Feel the heat of your breath as it fills up your lungs and the warmth of the blood running through your body.

2. Become aware of how the element of fire manifests in your environment and in nature. Take note of how fire appears in your electric appliances, candles, bonfires, and the warmth of the sun. Visualize fire burning in the Earth's core, in magma underneath its surface, and in lava pouring from volcanoes all across the world.

3. Mentally or out loud, call upon the collective energy of fire and the fire dragons. You can say, *I call upon the collective oversoul of fire and the fire dragons to come into my presence to shield my aura and transmute incoming negative energy.*

4. As you say this, you may notice the presence of fire dragons flying above your head, or even the presence of your dragon guardian from the element of fire coiling around your body. Take some time to make your acquaintance with the dragons and thank them in advance for the shielding.

5. Ask the dragons to blow their divine fire around the periphery of your aura with the aim of creating an impenetrable shield that transmutes incoming energy, protecting your light and keeping your vibration high.

6. After the process has finished, take some time to offer gratitude to the dragons, and when you feel ready, come out of the meditation.

Water Shield

Water's energy is fluid, dense, and pervasive. When you shield yourself with it, the energy permeates through every molecule of your energy field, leaving no room for incoming toxic energy attachments. Just like fire, water creates and destroys energy and can therefore transmute energy attack into positive energy. Think of how the ocean's waves erode the coast and form beaches with their tireless swashing and backwashing, how the rising and falling tides continuously reshape the coastline, or how rainfall can both nurture the land and create landslides that destroy part of it.

What differentiates water from fire is the *way* it transmutes energy. Fire is masculine; it consumes negative energy, burning it down to psychic dust until it transforms into something positive, just like the phoenix rising from the ashes. Water, on the other hand, is feminine; it neutralizes the negative energy rather than destroying it, allowing it to transform alchemically into something positive.

As a result, water shields are great to use when you experience psychic attack, such as when you interact with someone who's angry at or jealous of you, when you get bullied, and when you're under attack of any sort. The soothing, neutralizing energy of water will drown these angry, fiery emotions and transform them into love, keeping you safe in a protective bubble of calmness and peacefulness, just like the surface of a still lake.

Follow these steps to cast a water shield:

1. Closing your eyes, come into a meditative state. As you take long, deep breaths, notice how the element of water manifests in your body. Swallow a few times and become aware of the water in your saliva, feel the blood running through your veins keeping you alive and vital, and get a sense of your bodily fluids that keep your body flexible and agile.

2. Expand your awareness to see how the element of water manifests around you and in nature. Notice the water in the air you breathe, the presence of and accessibility of water in your house's appliances. Expand your vision further to observe the water in

the clouds, in rain, in the various streams, rivers, and lakes of our planet, as well as the water stored in ice and in the oceans shaping the land.

3. Mentally or out loud, call upon the collective energy of water and the water mermaids. You can say, *I call upon the collective oversoul of water and the water mermaids to come into my presence to shield my aura and transmute incoming negative energy.*

4. As you say this, you may notice the presence of water mermaids swimming around you or even the presence of your mermaid guardian from the element of water sideling toward your feet. Take some time to make your acquaintance with the mermaids and thank them in advance for the shielding.

5. Ask the mermaids to channel the powerful, recalibrating energy of water through your body and all around your aura in both a clockwise and counterclockwise direction, creating a dense energetic shield that transmutes incoming energy attacks into the purely positive energy of love.

6. After the process has finished, take some time to offer gratitude to the mermaids, and when you feel ready, come out of the meditation.

CHAPTER 30

Crystal Shields

My love of crystals started when I was seventeen years old. My best friend and I had just started on our spiritual journey, and every weekend we'd meet and hang out at the local crystal shop. Even at that young age, I was fascinated by the Earth's healing and protective qualities, and I'd spend hours looking at all the various crystals, reading the little information cards about their properties, and coming up with ways I could use them in my life.

I remember using rose quartz crystals to activate the feng shui love and relationships corner of my room and successfully manifesting a boyfriend shortly thereafter. I'd also read in a book that lapis lazuli was a great crystal for memory and performance, so I'd keep it near me during tests and exams at school. Crystals had quickly become my best friends, and I'd always carry a different one with me depending on the situation I was in, and I'd give advice freely to friends and family (even to my suspicious history teacher who thought I'd tried to cheat during a test by writing notes under my lapis lazuli!).

Over time, as I read, researched, and worked with various crystals, I was amazed at not just the number of uses they had but also the diversity of ways we could utilize them. Aside from using them as touchstones to support us in various activities, like I did when I first started working with them, we can use them to create crystal elixirs and mists, to set up energetic grids for manifestation and protection purposes, as Earth medicine to heal geopathic stress in toxic areas, and to cast energetic shields of protection around ourselves, others, and physical spaces.

My favorite way of working with crystals for energy protection is the latter, and this is the process I'll guide you through in this chapter.

Crystals for Energy Protection

Crystals have been used for energy protection for thousands of years. According to Judy Hall in her book *Crystals for Energy Protection*:

> *Recipes for crystal protection have been found that are over 5,000 years old and the same crystals are still being used today. Bloodstone, Hematite and Carnelian, for instance, were placed around the wrists of newborn babies in Mesopotamia and Egypt to ensure a long, prosperous and safe life, and the same combination is still effective in modern times. In the Neolithic period—"the Stone Age"—stones literally were the modern technology of the time. There is evidence from graves over 40,000 years old that crystals were used to protect the dead on their journey to the next world and we can assume that they were also used to protect the living.*[3]

When reading about the popularity and prevalence of crystals through the years, you may find yourself wondering what it is about them that makes them so useful—not just for energy protection, but for other purposes, too.

Although science hasn't fully explained the healing power of crystals, definite evidence points toward their healing properties. Specifically, quartz crystals are known to create *piezoelectricity*. When under pressure, they release a gentle electrical charge that's stable, accurate, and consistent; thus, they're used widely in watches, computers, and other technological tools. These stable electrical currents also interact with the unstable, ever-changing state of the human body, allowing us to synchronize with their vibration. This is known as the process of *entrainment*, during which a person synchronizes with an external influence that affects the way they think, feel, and behave.

Science has also already proven the power that colors have in affecting us both physically and emotionally; therefore, we can use crystals' vibrant colors to work with color energy to shift our mood. Think about how calm you usually feel when you're surrounded by soft shades of green and blue out in a forest or near the ocean, and compare this to the energizing qualities of hues of red and orange. When it comes to energy protection specifically, dark or black colors, such as the ones found in tourmaline and smoky quartz, have an internal lattice that traps energy within it, thus they're great at absorbing negative energy.

Although science is still in the early stages of explaining the full spectrum of crystals' healing qualities, history, experience, and metaphysical research suggests that crystals are powerful healing and protective tools. There are over five thousand identified crystals on planet Earth, each holding its own unique set of qualities. When we use them mindfully and with intention, we can partner with the crystals' vibrational qualities to create healing and transformation in our lives.

What Are Crystal Shields?

A *crystal shield* is when you work with a specific crystal, or a group of crystals, to create a shield around your aura that protects you from negative energy attachments. Since there are many different types of crystals, each with their own unique qualities, crystal shields can be amplifying, repelling, or transmuting. Some crystals can help amplify your energetic defenses and raise your vibration, such as rose quartz, celestite, and carnelian; others can absorb or repel energy, such as black tourmaline, hematite, and obsidian; and others can transmute energy, like shungite, labradorite, and smoky quartz.

A great variety of crystals also help clear your energy, such as quartz, amber, and orgonite. You can use these crystals to create cleansing crystal sprays and elixirs, as instructed in Chapter 22.

Rather than providing you with an extensive list of crystals belonging to each category, I'll instead provide a short list of the crystals that I use for various purposes. As with essential oils, it's important that you do your own research and trust your intuition when choosing crystals to work with. Despite the crystals' known qualities, which you can find in crystal books and other resources, they work in different ways with different people, so a crystal that works in a certain way for me may work differently for you.

From an energetic standpoint, crystals can focus, store, repel, transmit, or transform energy, and each crystal has one or more of these properties. For the purpose of energy shielding, we're more interested in the transmitting, storing/repelling, and transforming properties of crystals, which correspond to the three types of shields introduced in Chapter 25: amplifying, repelling, and transmuting.

Here's my list of crystals associated with the three types of shields:

Amplifying Crystals

- **Celestite:** Helps you raise your vibration by connecting to the angels and the higher realms.

- **Rose Quartz:** Opens your heart chakra to allow unconditional love from Source to saturate your whole being.

- **Carnelian:** Heals and recalibrates your body and boosts your immune system.

- **Citrine:** Helps you acknowledge and express your confidence and willpower.

- **Selenite:** Uses crystalized divine light to repair wounds and holes in your aura and energy field.

Repelling/Absorbing Crystals

- **Black Tourmaline:** Repels incoming energy attack and absorbs negative energy from the environment.

- **Aventurine:** Protects and preserves your life-force energy when you're dealing with energy vampires.

⊛ **Hematite:** Creates an impenetrable shield that prevents negative energies from entering your energy field. It also reframes your beliefs around boundaries so that you make choices that uphold your energetic authenticity.

⊛ **Black Obsidian:** Absorbs negative energy and holds it within its internal lattice. Needs to be cleared frequently.

Transmuting Crystals

⊛ **Shungite:** Strengthens your energy immune system and casts a shield of protective light around your aura that clears and purifies incoming toxic energy.

⊛ **Smoky Quartz:** Filters negative energy from the environment to ensure that what comes in is clear and pure.

⊛ **Labradorite:** Creates a subtle transmuting shield that allows you to filter incoming toxic energy from others while still being able to connect and communicate empathically.

⊛ **Lapis Lazuli:** Clears and reverses conscious or unconscious psychic attacks from your energy field while tending to the energetic wounds that resulted from the attacks.

How to Cast a Crystal Shield

Follow this process to cast a crystal shield:

1. Choose your crystal or selection of crystals. If you're just starting out working with crystals, it's best to choose a single crystal that possesses the protective qualities you need at this time.

2. Cleanse your crystals either by running them through cold water (ensure the crystals aren't water soluble), by energetically washing them in a plume of smoke, or by placing them in dry rice for twenty-four hours (don't consume the rice afterward because it'll contain the negative energy it absorbed from the crystals).

3. Energize your crystals by either placing them in sunlight for at least three hours or by sending them rainbow light as instructed in Chapter 22.

4. When your crystals are cleansed and energized, you're ready to program them for shielding. Hold your chosen crystal near your heart, close your eyes, and come into a meditative state. Call upon the collective essence of the crystal to make itself present. To do so, visualize underground mountains of your chosen crystal and feel the collective essence of that crystal activating the one in your hand. Once you've made contact with the crystal's collective essence, say something along the lines of *I call upon the collective presence of [name of crystal] to flow through this crystal and cast a protective shield around my energy. Thank you for keeping me safe and protected for as long as I need.*

5. Visualize the energy of the crystal from within your hand radiating outward to infuse your body and aura with its protective qualities. Depending on your intuition language, you may see a specific color, feel a certain emotion, hear some kind of sound, or just know that the crystal shield is in place.

6. When you feel yourself surrounded by this protective cocoon of crystal light, thank the crystal for its help and end the meditation. You can either carry the crystal with you throughout the day to help maintain the shield, or place it on your altar and know that the spirit of the crystal will remain with you, shielding and protecting you.

CHAPTER 31

Shielding with Essential Oils

*E*ssential oils are oils derived from several plant parts, including leaves, seeds, roots, flowers, stems, rhizomes, berries, needles, bark, wood, and rinds. Obtained via steam distillation or expression (pressing), essential oils are 75–100 percent more concentrated than the plant from which they're obtained, which makes them highly potent for physical, emotional, mental, and spiritual healing.

Essential oils have been used for millennia for medicines, perfumes, cosmetics, and culinary purposes. In recent years, the therapeutic qualities of essential oils have been studied under the modality of aromatherapy, with an increased number of scientific studies corroborating their effectiveness.

Traditionally, essential oils are inhaled or applied topically to alleviate a number of symptoms. Spiritually, and for the purpose of energy protection, we can leverage the protective qualities of the collective spirit or oversoul of the oil's plant to cast protective shields. Similar to crystals, the protective power and qualities of essential oils depend on the plant they're derived from, so you can use essential oils to cast all kinds of shields, including those that amplify, repel, and transmute.

Working with Plant Spirits

Using essential oils for energy protection allows you to work with plant spirits and elementals in a tangible and multisensory way, which may amplify the protective capacity of the shielding process. When you work with essential oils, you come in direct contact with the physical, aromatic, chemical, and spiritual components of a plant. As mentioned in earlier chapters, although the physical aspect of nature isn't necessary to leveraging its protective qualities, we perceive that from our human standpoint, which strengthens the protective experience.

Each plant, tree, and flower carries unique healing and protective qualities that are held within, and we can access these qualities through its essential oil. The very term *essential oil* suggests that the oil holds the very essence of the plant, giving you access to not just the chemical components of the specific plant used to create the oil, but also the collective spirit of the whole plant species. Therefore, when you use essential oils for energy shielding, you leverage the protective qualities of the entire collective plant consciousness.

Essential Oils for Energy Protection

As with crystals, it's important that you do your own research and trust your intuition when it comes to picking essential oils for energy protection. We all respond to different essential oils in different ways, and so do different types of energy attachments. The following list includes essential oils traditionally associated with energy protection as well as the ones that I personally use to cast various protective shields.

- **Amplifying shield oils:** Rose, rose geranium, lemon verbena, ylang ylang, myrtle, bergamot, sweet orange, jasmine, chamomile
- **Repelling shield oils:** Cedarwood, thyme, rosemary, pine needle, sage, black pepper
- **Transmuting shield oils:** Lavender, neroli, frankincense, eucalyptus, peppermint

In addition to working with single-plant oils, you may also choose to use an essential oil blend that you make yourself or purchase one from a reputable essential oil brand. Many essential oil blends made exclusively for energy protection are sold by various companies.

Using an essential oil blend is ideal when you want to utilize the healing and protective qualities of multiple plants, such as when you require the amplifying qualities of one oil and the repelling qualities of another. By finding the essential oil combination that works best for you, you can then use just this blend for your daily shielding practice.

Using Essential Oils Safely

Before you proceed with the following process, it's important to consider the following safety measures:

- Due to their high concentrations, essential oils can irritate or burn your skin when applied undiluted. Apart from a few oils which can be applied to the skin undiluted, most essential oils must be diluted in a base oil, such as almond or coconut oil. One or two drops of essential oil in a fifteen milliliter bottle is a safe dilution to start with, but always do a patch test by applying a small amount of the essential oil on your skin before you work with essential oils in the following process.

- Citrus oils such as bergamot, lime, lemon, and grapefruit are phototoxic, meaning that they can irritate your skin if you apply them and then expose yourself to the sun. It's best to avoid using these oils if you're about to spend time in the sun and ensure that you wash your hands thoroughly after using them.

- Always research the safety requirements of the essential oil you're about to work with by referring to reputable essential oils books and online resources. Search for the essential oil's monograph online to get accurate scientific information.

How to Cast an Essential Oil Shield

Follow these steps to shield yourself with essential oils:

1. After choosing your diluted essential oil, hold the bottle in front of your chest and call upon the collective spirit or oversoul of your chosen plant. You can say something along the lines of *I call upon the collective essence of [name of plant] to flow through this blend and empower it with its protective qualities.* As you say this, visualize field upon field of your chosen plant in its natural habitat. You may see the plant's spirit showing up as a deity or simply feel its presence with you.

2. At this point, you've got the entire plant species consciousness present with, and ready to protect, you. With reverence, pour three drops of the oil on your palms and rub them together. Placing your hands in the prayer position, lift your hands to your face and inhale three times, taking in the essence of the oil. By doing this, you benefit from the aromatic qualities of the oil, and you also embody the protective essence of the oil's spirit.

3. Extend your hands and palms outward and wave them around your body and aura, visualizing protective light extending from your palms and creating a light bubble around your aura. Depending on the protective qualities of your chosen plant, your shield may amplify your existing defenses or create a repelling or transmuting auric layer.

4. After you've shielded yourself with the oil's presence, take a minute or two to bask in the safety of the plant spirit, asking it to stay with you and protect you throughout the day or for as long as you need it to.

CHAPTER 32

Breath of Fire

*B*reath of fire is a fast-breathing meditation that can help you amplify your natural auric defenses. It's a great process to use when you're not surrounded by much negativity and just require a basic process that strengthens your natural auric defenses and keeps your vibration high. Breath of fire, also known as *Agni Pran*, is one of the foundational breathing techniques in Kundalini Yoga.

I first experienced this technique during a Kundalini Yoga practice of ego eradicator, and I was instantly hooked. By the end of the three-minute meditation, my entire body was vibrating, my aura had expanded and was pulsating, and I felt as high and energized as I feel after an hour-long meditation. Since then, I've guided people to use this process in my workshops and private sessions as a quick way to both recalibrate their energy and amplify their auric defenses.

Essentially, breath of fire is a fast, rhythmic, continuous breath from the nostrils, with the mouth closed. You breathe equally in the inhale and the exhale with no pauses in between. The breath is powered from the diaphragm and solar plexus, so that the upper abdominal muscles expand on the inbreath and contract on the outbreath.

According to the creator of Kundalini Yoga, Yogi Bhajan, breath of fire has many health benefits, including strengthening our energetic protection.

Specifically, according to Yogi Bhajan, author of *The Aquarian Teacher*, breath of fire

- Releases toxins and deposits from the lungs, mucous linings, blood vessels, and other cells.
- Strengthens the nervous system to resist stress.
- Repairs the balance between the sympathetic and para-sympathetic nervous systems.
- Adjusts the subtle psycho-electromagnetic field of the aura so that the blood becomes energized.
- Boosts the immune system and may help prevent many diseases.
- Promotes synchronization of the biorhythms of the body's systems.[4]

Since our physical and energy immune systems are interconnected, by strengthening one, we automatically strengthen and empower the other, too.

Contraindications

While breath of fire is a safe process for most people, it can be risky for people with heart problems, high blood pressure, spinal disorders, respiratory problems, and vertigo, and should be avoided. This is also the case if you're pregnant or menstruating.

Use the following steps to amplify your auric defenses using breath of fire:

1. Sitting up straight, close your eyes and take a few deep breaths to center your energy.

2. Focusing on your solar plexus chakra, set a timer for one to three minutes and start breathing using breath of fire by following the previous breathing description. (You may want to watch a video online to ensure you're doing it right.)

3. While breathing, keep your attention on your solar plexus chakra and observe as your body's and aura's vibration naturally shifts. There's no need to consciously visualize something, just keep your mind calm and focused, and let the process work.

4. When you're done, stay in a meditative position for a few more minutes, taking deep breaths and basking in the energy.

CHAPTER 33

Violet Flame Shield

The *violet flame* is a high-vibrational energy that transmutes negative energy attachments into love and light. It's traditionally connected with Saint Germain and Archangel Zadkiel, but when I connect to it, I usually envision high-dimensional fire dragons carrying it. You will receive this energy from a source that makes sense to you, depending on your viewpoint. This flame is unlike the dragon fire you've used before to clear your etheric body since it works at a far higher frequency to transmute all forms of energy attack and negativity. Although it resembles the violet color of a rainbow ray, it has a completely distinct energy, which is why it's usually called a flame rather than light.

Despite the fact that both the violet flame and the rainbow ray have high vibrational frequencies, they express themselves in distinct ways and hence serve different purposes. The rainbow ray raises vibration whereas the violet flame transforms negative vibration. One activates, while the other transmutes.

During this process, you will shield yourself with a layer of violet flame to protect yourself from attracting energy attack as well as to cleanse and transmute any energy attachments you may have accumulated over the day. Because the violet flame clears and protects at the same time, it's a quick technique to utilize on a regular basis for both energy clearing and shielding.

Follow these steps to shield yourself using the violet flame:

1. Enter a meditative state and call upon the violet flame dragons and the element of fire. You could say, *I call upon the spirit of fire and the violet flame dragons to come into my presence and guide me through this process.*

2. The violet flame emanates from the ethers rather than the violet flame dragons. It exists right now, but in a separate dimension. The dragons just direct and lead the flow of energy; all you have to do is focus on and call upon it to activate it within you. When you're ready, say, *I call upon the violet flame to come into my presence now. Thank you for flowing through my body and spirit, transmuting all negativity, and protecting my energy throughout the day.*

3. The violet flame will appear within and around you. It will appear to be ordinary violet light at first, but the longer you stare at it, the more you'll discover it burns and sparkles like fire. Visualize the violet flame encompassing your body and aura, removing any lingering negativity. Rather than interfering with the rainbow ray, it cooperates with it to make you impervious to external negativity.

4. Once you've established the boundaries of the violet flame shield within and around you, give thanks for its protection and come out of meditation.

You can download an expanded audio recording of this meditation at *GeorgeLizos.com/PYL.*

CHAPTER 34

Golden Pyramid of Light Shield

While sitting in meditation one day, I felt the Greek god Apollo come into my presence and place a golden-light pyramid around my body. When I activated its five sides, I could feel the golden light seeping through my aura and body and almost instantly clearing and recalibrating my energy. Although I hadn't properly researched sacred geometry, by that point I knew that the pyramid was a powerful symbol for energy protection.

As I delved into the ancient texts to uncover the spiritual significance of pyramids and the triangle, I could clearly see why it was so potent. According to the ancient Greek mathematician Euclid, the triangle was the first primal shape and is the core of the elemental worlds. Specifically, in 360 BCE, Greek philosopher Plato theorized that an equilateral triangle creates five polyhedral shapes known as the *platonic solids*. According to Plato, these shapes represent the elements of earth, air, fire, water, and spirit, and they are the *core pattern* behind all physical creation. In the 1980s Professor Robert Moon, who taught at the University of Chicago, confirmed that the platonic solids are indeed the foundation for the arrangement of protons and neutrons in all the elements of the periodic table.[5]

A square pyramid made up of four triangles and a square base, identical to the famous Egyptian pyramids, provides the perfect structure for transmuting energy. Its stable square base is grounded firmly to the Earth while the four sides reach upward and meet in a single point. This creates a symbolic and energetic flow of energy from Earth to Heaven, and vice versa. Essentially, the pyramid acts as a bridge between the physical and spiritual worlds, allowing for Source Energy to flow through you from the top of the pyramid, to cleanse and recalibrate your energy, and then to ground and anchor that energy into the Earth.

Meditating within a physical pyramid structure is a great way to transmute toxic energy attachments and raise your vibration, but you can get the same results by mentally casting a pyramid shield around your body. Although you can shield yourself with whichever pyramid color makes the most sense to you, casting a golden pyramid shield will make your shield impenetrable. Gold is the color associated with Source; spiritually, it has the highest vibrational frequency of all colors and can attune you to the frequency of your inner being almost instantly.

Use the following steps to cast a golden pyramid shield:

1. Close your eyes and come into a meditative state. Focus on your crown chakra and the top of your head, your communication portal with Source and the higher realms. Setting your intention to shield yourself with the golden light of Source, see a golden ball of light start to shine through your crown chakra. Invite this light to bathe your physical body and aura, and with every breath, visualize it flowing through you and saturating every part of your being.

2. When you've infused your entire body and aura with the golden light from your crown chakra, let that golden light take the shape of a golden pyramid that envelops your body. To make this extra powerful, call upon Apollo, the Greek god of light and energy protection, to support the process. Ensure that the pyramid has four triangular sides and a square base.

3. The pyramid emits golden light both inward and outward. The inward-facing light transmutes energy attachments already

present within your being, while the outward-facing light transmutes incoming energy attachments, ensuring that what comes in is loving and high vibe. Spend some time basking within the golden pyramid, letting its light transmute toxic energy within and without your energy field.

4. Program the pyramid to stay lit up throughout the day, or for as long as you need it, to keep transmuting incoming negative energy.

5. Stay in this meditative state for as long as you wish, and when you feel complete, come out of the meditation.

You can download an expanded audio recording of this meditation at *GeorgeLizos.com/PYL.*

CHAPTER 35

Shielding with Amulets and Talismans

A mulets and talismans are symbols and objects, usually worn around the neck as pendants or held somewhere on the body, that are used to protect against energy attacks. Although the two terms are often used interchangeably, there are key distinctions between them.

Amulets are traditionally associated with warding off negative energy, and therefore they create a repelling energy shield around your aura that protects against energy attack. As explained by Roman natural philosopher Pliny the Elder in his book *Natural History*, an amulet is "an object that protects a person from trouble." *Talismans*, on the other hand, have amplifying qualities and aim to strengthen the natural energy defenses of the person who wears them. Anything can be used to create amulets and talismans, with some of the most popular objects being crystals, statues, coins, drawings, and written words.

Both amulets and talismans have been used since antiquity, and are still used today, by many cultures around the world. In Egypt, pregnant women would wear amulets portraying Tauret, the goddess of pregnancy and childbirth, to protect them against miscarriage. The ancient Greeks and Romans associated gods and goddesses with crystals and created amulets and talismans made of chalcedony, jasper, and amethyst, whereas in China, the Taoist *fulu* was a special style of calligraphy used to protect against evil spirits.

Presently, amulets and talismans are still used profusely throughout the world as part of religion as well as popular belief. The Turkish *nazar*, a circular, blue-glass eye, is a great example of an amulet used to protect against the evil eye primarily in West Asian countries, while the crucifix is another popular amulet used by Christians to protect against ill-wishing and other negative entities. Other popular objects used as amulets and talismans through the years have been garlic, coal, runes, lucky coins, and horseshoes.

How Amulets and Talismans Work

Like all energy protection tools and processes, amulets' and talismans' protective abilities depend on the intention, beliefs, prayers, and blessings bestowed on them. What distinguishes them from most energy protection tools—aside from the fact that you're working with something tangible—is the combined, and often collective, intentionality that goes into their creation. Amulets and talismans leverage their protective abilities from the combined prayers, beliefs, and intentions of the people who created and use them.

For example, if you choose to use a talisman that you've bought or that was gifted to you by someone, that talisman will hold the protective qualities instilled in it by the person who created it in addition to the protective qualities of your own intentions. Simultaneously, when you are wearing popular amulets such as the nazar or a crucifix, the amulet holds the collective protective qualities of all the people who have used that specific amulet for protection in the past and present. Due to the collaborative nature of amulets' and talismans' protective qualities, it's important that you fully trust the person or people that contributed to their creation, and the collective intentionality behind them, before you start using them.

From an energetic perspective, the amulet or talisman casts a protective energy shield around your aura, performing its programmed qualities. Although both amulets' and talismans' protective shields are quite lasting, they require frequent reprogramming to maintain their effectiveness. I've heard many stories of people's nazars breaking unexpectedly and spontaneously when exposed to intense negativity. This happens when the amulet has not been recharged or reprogrammed for a while, has thus lost its repelling or amplifying qualities, and has, as a result, not been able to withstand the incoming energy attack.

Creating an Amulet or Talisman

Although there's great benefit to purchasing an amulet or talisman, especially when it's made specifically for you, I prefer to create my own. Although there's nothing wrong with letting others support our energy-protecting efforts, depending solely on someone else's intentions and power for our own protection can easily lead to codependent patterns that rid us of our power. Conversely, when we take the time to create our own protective amulets and talismans, we acknowledge and honor our power to protect our energy, which is in and of itself a powerful protection tool.

Use the following steps to create your own amulet or talisman:

1. First, choose whether you'd like to create an amulet or a talisman. Remember that an amulet repels energy attacks whereas a talisman amplifies your natural energy defenses. If you want, you may create an object that combines both qualities, or even a transmuting talisman. Don't let the terms limit you, and allow yourself to create something that works for you.

2. Come into a meditative state and go through the steps of connecting with your protection guide, as explained in Chapter 8. Feeling centered, grounded, and connected, ask your guide to inspire you with a symbol or an object that will act as your

amulet or talisman. Stay in meditation for a few minutes and let this symbol or object take form.

3. If it's a symbol, be sure to draw it on paper right away so you don't forget it. You can also draw your symbol on a piece of wood, clay, stone, or crystal. If it's not a symbol, follow the instructions you've received to create it. The most powerful amulets and talismans are either completely made out of natural materials or are a combination of ready-made physical tokens and natural materials.

4. Before you use your chosen items, be sure to clear their energy by running them under cold water or through smoke.

5. Having crafted your amulet or talisman, hold it in front of your chest and program it with intention, prayer, and/or by calling upon your protection guide and other guides to add their protective powers. You can say something along the lines of *I ask this amulet to cast a repelling shield of light around my body and aura to ward off negative energy for as long as I wear it. Thank you [name of your chosen guide] for infusing the amulet with your protective qualities, keeping me safe and protected at all times.*

6. To consolidate your programming, you may want to anoint your amulet or talisman with an essential oil you feel has the qualities you want to infuse it with, and blow at it, or give it a kiss, to infuse it with your energy.

7. You're now ready to use your amulet or talisman. You can either wear it on a daily basis or just when you feel like you need its specific protective qualities. To sustain its protection powers, it's a good idea to reprogram it before each use.

Tips for Buying Amulets and Talismans

You may choose to buy an amulet or talisman rather than create one yourself, or you may be gifted one by a healer or friend. As mentioned earlier, amulets and talismans created by others, or popular commercial ones that have been used over time by many people, can provide additional protective power that draws from the collective intentionality that went into their creation. However, not all amulets and talismans created by others are safe to use, and not all popular ones are right for everyone.

Follow these guidelines when buying or when you are gifted an amulet or talisman:

- **Learn more about its creator:** Find out about the creator and intention behind your chosen amulet or talisman. Was it created by a single person or by a group of people? What is that person's/group's training? What kind of ritual practices were used in its creation? Do you agree with the person's/group's spiritual beliefs and worldview? If you're buying your amulet or talisman from an occult shop, you can ask the shop owner to give you more information about this. If that's not sufficient, hold the amulet or talisman in your hands, tune in to your intuition, and see what you receive. How does your body respond to it? Do you feel an expansion or a contraction at the idea of using it?

- **Study the symbols:** Does the amulet or talisman depict any symbols? A *symbol* is a sign, shape, or object that stands for something else. Symbols used by many people over many years contain coded information, archetypes, thought forms, and emotions, all related to the symbol's collective use. Before you choose an amulet or talisman, do some research on the symbol it portrays and ensure that it resonates with your belief system and that you'd want it as your ally.

- **Make it your own:** If you end up buying a commercial, factory-made amulet such as a nazar or a crucifix, be aware that its protective energy draws mostly from its collective use and intentionality over the years rather than from the person who facilitated its creation. Provided that you resonate with the collective programming behind the amulet or talisman, the fact that it's not one of a kind and is produced en masse gives you the opportunity to make it your own and infuse it with your own intention. To do so, follow steps 4 to 7 in the previous section to clear, program, and anoint it.

If you end up with an amulet or talisman that you don't vibe with, pass it along to someone who'll put it to better use or dispose of it by burying it into the earth.

CHAPTER 36

Shielding with Your Spirit Guides

As you've probably realized by experimenting with the various shielding techniques I've introduced so far, there are countless ways you can leverage your intention, imagination, nature, and various sources of light and energy to shield and protect yourself. Energy protection has been practiced by many cultures for thousands of years, and you can work with innumerable techniques, processes, and energies.

In this book, I've chosen to include the ones I've personally used and have found to work well for this time and age. Aside from the elementals, I haven't introduced techniques related to other spirit guides, such as angels, saints, departed loved ones, animal spirits, star people, and ascended masters. I've done this consciously to honor everyone's spiritual beliefs and to keep the book as nondenominational as possible. However, this part wouldn't be complete without introducing the benefits of working with such spirit guides, whatever form they may take or whichever religion they're related to.

Spirit guides are personal or collective deities that accompany and guide us through our journey on planet Earth. Some guides are given to us at birth and accompany us throughout our lives, whereas others come and go depending on our needs and desires. Personal guides work exclusively with us for the duration of our lives and beyond, while collective guides work with multiple people at the same time.

Different cultures, religions, and spiritual paths work with different spirit guides, and it's important to go through your own personal journey of meeting and choosing the ones that you feel guided to. In this chapter, I'll share general guidelines for connecting and working with your chosen spirit guides for energy shielding.

My Spirit Guides Journey

My spiritual beliefs have shifted over the years. Growing up Christian, I used to call upon Jesus, Mother Mary, and various other saints for protection. I later experimented with witchcraft during which I relied mostly on protective amulets, talismans, and the energies of nature. When I transitioned to New Age, I trained in Angel Therapy and worked with various angels, archangels, and ascended masters for protection. Now, having transitioned to Greek Paganism, I often call upon the elementals and various Greek gods and goddesses, such as Apollo, Zeus, and Aphrodite.

What was interesting about working with these seemingly contrasting spirit guides was that they all helped me equally well to protect my energy. This further supports my statement that it is our intention and our belief in a process that are the primary factors that make a process work rather than the process itself. Source Energy expresses in as many ways as there are people on this planet, and more. As a result, Source will find a way to work with us and protect us based on our current belief system. I've always believed that there are many pathways to Source, and this is also true for energy protection.

Benefits of Working with Spirit Guides

Rather than providing you with a list of deities and spirit guides that you can work with for energy shielding, I want you to turn to your own spiritual belief system, tradition, or religion for guidance. Who do you feel is an appropriate spirit guide to work with for energy shielding? Is it an archangel, a pagan god or goddess, an ascended master, your spirit animal, a departed loved one, your star family, or an elemental? Furthermore, which spirit guide feels right to help you execute the various shielding processes I introduced in this part? If you don't have a strong association to any spiritual tradition, you can always continue working with your energy protection guardian who you met in Chapter 8 to guide and strengthen your shielding practice.

That being said, you don't necessarily need to call upon specific spirit guides when clearing or shielding your energy. Your own personal power and intention are enough to protect you. If you do have strong beliefs and connections to specific spirit guides, though, leveraging their support and protective qualities will be incredibly beneficial. Since all spirit guides are extensions of you, connecting with them can be a catalyst for accessing unexpressed parts of yourself, speeding up your ascension journey and helping you reach your highest spiritual potential.

Concurrently, when you are connecting with your spirit guides for the purpose of shielding your energy, they may introduce new shielding techniques that are personalized to you. I've often called upon Aphrodite when I'm feeling insecure or uneasy during dates, Zeus when I'm feeling lost or scared, and Apollo when I'm feeling psychically attacked by someone. In all cases, the gods and goddess came in and shielded me with their unique energies or guided me through more complex processes of energy protection. You can do the same by experimenting with the deities you feel a close connection to.

Use the following meditation to shield yourself with the help of your chosen spirit guides:

1. Close your eyes and come into a meditative state. Go through the process of centering and grounding yourself, and open yourself up to connect with your chosen spirit guide. You can call upon either your energy protection guardian or any other spirit guide you wish to work with.

2. To secure the connection, mentally or out loud say something along the lines of *I call upon [name of spirit guide] to come into my presence and shield my energy field. Thank you for protecting me against toxic energy of all forms, keeping me aligned to love and light.*

3. At this point, you'll feel the energy of your guide come into your presence. Use your dominant intuition language to connect with them, and ask them to show you the best way to protect yourself.

4. What will happen next will be completely up to your spirit guide. You may see them shielding you with light, gifting you an energetic amulet or talisman, or guiding you through a visualization or a different process. The possibilities are endless. Be present and connected and let your guide lead the way.

5. Once the process is complete, offer your gratitude to your spirit guide and ask them to stay with you, upholding the protection for as long as you need it. When you're done, come out of the meditation feeling safe and protected.

CHAPTER 37

Energy Shielding FAQs

You may find yourself asking questions about the effectiveness, usefulness, and frequency of practice as you experiment with these energy shielding processes, as well as other processes you may have learned along the way. The four most common questions about energy shielding that I receive are as follows:

Are These Processes Foolproof?

All of the processes I've described are powerful and effective in protecting you from energy attack, but they're not foolproof. They're only as effective as your vibrational frequency allows them to be in the present moment. Your vibrational frequency rises and falls as you go through the different experiences of your day. Yes, the rainbow ray keeps it high, but you have the power to diminish or enhance its potency by focusing on life's negative experiences.

As a result, while the rainbow ray and violet flame will shield you from psychic attack to a large extent, as your vibration oscillates, you may still attract negativity.

Can I Use These Shielding Processes in Combination with Others?

Yes, you don't need to change your energy shielding practice if it's effective. However, I recommend that you try these methods at least once to see how well they work for you. You may come to prefer them to your current processes, or they may even inspire you to create a new one.

How Often Should I Shield Myself?

In an ideal world, you should shield yourself every morning with the intention of keeping the protection for the entire day. Given that your vibrational frequency will inevitably change throughout the day, it's safer to shield yourself again in the middle of the day to supplement your existing shields.

Simultaneously, simply by intending it, you can strengthen or reactivate your shields if you ever feel vulnerable to external negativity. When I'm in a hospital, a gym, an airport, or anywhere else where there's a large group of people, I'll often shield myself. My shoulders relax and my mood improves almost immediately when I do so.

When Should I Strengthen My Protective Shields?

I've talked about some of the occasions during which you'd want to strengthen your protective shields and the specific shields associated with them, in their respective sections. Here's a more comprehensive list of such occasions:

 ● **When you're feeling disconnected from Source**

   As I mentioned earlier, the degree to which you attract energy attack depends on the degree to which you're aligned to your inner being. When your vibrational frequency is high, meaning that you're mostly feeling positive emotions, then you're naturally aligned to Source and you can only attract people, energies, and experiences at that high vibrational state.

You only become vulnerable to attack when your vibrational frequency is lower than the frequency of your inner being. From this perspective, anytime you feel like you're disconnected from Source is a good time to amplify your spiritual practice and energy protection shields to bring yourself back into a place of alignment.

ø When you're caught up in a toxic interaction

We've all been in a position of being stuck at a gathering with toxic people who are sharing the dramas and traumas of their day-to-day lives. The energy in the room gets increasingly heavy and overwhelming, and we leave the gathering feeling drained and disheartened. Although it's important to be empathetic, it's also important to ensure we don't take on these people's energy.

My suggestion for dealing with such toxic interactions is to politely leave. If, for whatever reason, you're not able to leave, then this is the time to strengthen your shields to protect your auric field and secure your energy.

ø During and after illness

When we go through periods of physical illness, surgery, or any form of mental health issue, our energy field gets scarred and weakened. Since our mental and physical health is directly linked to our energetic health, it's vital that we take the time to both clear and shield our energy more diligently. This won't just protect you from attracting energy attack of any form, but it'll also help you heal faster.

ø When you are traveling or are surrounded by many people

It's important to take extra time shielding yourself before you go to airports, hospitals, or entertainment venues such as cinemas, concerts, clubs, shopping centers, or even the town farmer's market. Whenever you're surrounded by a large group of people, you're automatically vulnerable to their energy field interacting with yours, or to them consciously or unconsciously sending negative energy toward you. If you're a sensitive empath, you'll likely feel heavier and depleted after a long day in such places, even if you haven't done much and have had a relaxing day. This is a result of your aura being inundated with energy attachments from both people and spaces.

⊛ **Whenever you feel like it**

Sometimes, you may feel the need to strengthen your protective shields even if there's no apparent reason to do so. Trust that feeling and do what it takes to make yourself feel safe. As you've learned in this book, there are many different levels of energy attack, and although your conscious mind may not recognize all of them, your intuition always picks up on them.

PART IV

Protecting Your Energy Online

CHAPTER 38

Living in a Digital Landscape

One of the reasons energy protection has become such a crucial skill to develop is due to our increasing exposure to people and places, not just offline, but also in the digital spaces we inhabit. Technological advances have helped us drop the boundaries of time and space and have made traveling around the world cheaper and faster; they've done the same for the online spaces we hang out in. Over the past few decades, we've progressively transitioned our lives and businesses online; more and more people are getting comfortable interacting with each other, and working, online. The COVID-19 pandemic has been a catalyst for the digital revolution, making living and working online unavoidable.

What's important to understand about online spaces is that they are indeed *spaces*. Although they're immaterial, they exist virtually and carry energy in a similar way to the way physical spaces do. In the words of Katie Brockhurst in her book *Social Media for a New Age 2*:

> It's a digital world, a sprawling metropolis, that keeps changing
> and growing. New highways are built and roads are re-routed,
> new suburbs pop up in the form of features and updates . . .
> Then there are all the people, the adverts and videos that show
> up in our timelines through sponsored posts and ads. Knocking

*on our digital doors everyday often unannounced or uninvited,
is like having the double-glazing sales men, a Jehovah's witness,
plus all of the marketing and sales leaflets dropping through your
letterbox and knocking at your door all at the same time.*[6]

As a result, it's important that we take the time to understand the digital spaces we interact in so we can take the necessary measures to protect ourselves and our energy. Although digital spaces function similarly to physical spaces energetically, and thus many of the clearing and shielding processes you've learned so far in this book will also help you protect yourself online, there are important nuances and specific processes that will help deepen your protection. In this last part of the book, we'll explore the nature of digital spaces and the way we interact in them, and then I'll share both tactical and spiritual tips and processes to help you protect your energy online.

Understanding Digital Spaces

Think of the digital landscape as a world existing within a world. First, we have the physical world we inhabit, with its various continents, countries, cities, houses, and all the human and spiritual interactions and flows that occur throughout it. We have public spaces such as streets, parks, and town centers; semi-public spaces such as shopping centers, cinemas, restaurants, and bars; and private spaces such as our homes and vehicles.

Then, we have the digital world that exists in a parallel dimension within, and essentially mirroring, the physical world. Various social media platforms can be seen as different countries, each with their own set of public and private spaces in which we can interact.

Let's take Instagram as an example: the Explore tab and the various hashtag hubs are akin to public spaces in big cities; you can scroll through and encounter all kinds of people, information, and energies. Your newsfeed on Instagram is a semi-public space where you're still exposed to a wide variety of content, primarily from people you've chosen to hear from.

Finally, your DM section is a private space in which you can have more intimate conversations with people you choose to engage with. Similar to Instagram, Facebook, Twitter, LinkedIn, TikTok, Snapchat, YouTube, WhatsApp, and other social media platforms are all digital countries with their own set of public, semi-public, and private spaces.

Engaging in multiple platforms is very similar to being a popstar on a world tour flying from country to country, giving concerts, meeting fans, and doing interviews. Your physical body may be at home, lounging on the couch and enjoying a hot cup of cocoa while scrolling on your phone, but your subtle bodies (your emotional, mental, and sometimes your astral bodies) are globetrotting the digital world. Although your physical body may be shielded and protected, your other bodies may be exposed to all kinds of energies that they encounter in their digital travels.

Communicating Online

In my experience, online communication makes us more vulnerable to energy attack than face-to-face communication. In the real world, we use our senses to scan our surrounding environment and gauge its energy before we enter it. Once we're in, we also use our senses, and especially our auric attraction, to engage with people who we feel we're going to have a pleasant interaction with. If we end up in a conversation with someone we don't vibe with, we sense that promptly and can turn around and leave if we wish to.

With online conversations, communication is stripped down to words, and sometimes emojis, that unsuccessfully attempt to mimic the plethora and complexity of human emotions. By losing the physical aspect of communication—the physical presence, emotions, energy, and nonverbal cues—we also lose part of our capacity to scan the digital space and gauge the quality of people and our interactions with them. Although we can definitely learn to humanize our textual conversations with the right use of language and emojis, and by including audio and visual messages, we still inevitably lose a big part of human communication.

Many people choose to use the dehumanized nature of digital communication to act out of character and communicate in a harsher and more unhindered way that doesn't truly reflect their character. Others choose to alter or completely replace their identity by hiding behind fake pictures and profiles, and by interacting via a digital persona. Consequently, communicating in the digital space is vastly different than communicating in the physical world, which amplifies the ways through which we can be energetically attacked.

Energy Attack in Digital Spaces

Energy attack in the digital landscape works in the same way as it does in the physical world. Even if we're not in close proximity to the people we interact with and are exposed to on social media, we're still connected to them via the digital space we share. Our common presence in the same digital space gives them access to our energy and makes us vulnerable to attack. In the same way you're vulnerable to energy attack when you go out to a restaurant and expose yourself to strangers, you're equally vulnerable to attack when you enter a comment thread on a Facebook or Instagram post. Remember, digital spaces were created to mirror physical spaces, and they also mirror the way energy flows between the people who interact in them.

As a result, all the types of energy attack we mentioned in Chapter 5 can occur in the digital landscape and can include anything from attracting residual spatial energy from the social spaces we interact with to receiving psychic daggers of attack and jealousy.

A few years ago, I was a victim of energy attack in the form of psychic daggers while engaging with someone in the comments of a YouTube video. I'd made a comment about there being many spiritual paths to knowing Source; this was met by a judgmental comment from a dogmatic Christian who stated that there was only one true path to God. One comment led to the next, and an hour later, I was caught up in a full-fledged debate on dogma and religion. I left the interaction feeling drained and disheartened that we weren't able to find common ground. I subsequently deleted my comments in an effort to disconnect from the energy, but it was too late. That night I had an excruciating migraine and stomachache that kept me up all night.

Recent studies on the psychology of social media support the existence of energy attack online in what is referred to as the emotional contagion. The *emotional contagion* is defined as the way through which one person's or group of people's emotions can be transferred to and can trigger similar emotions in other people. Specifically, a recent experiment performed on Facebook showed that "emotions spread online, even in absence of non-verbal cues typical of in-person interactions, and that individuals are more likely to adopt positive or negative emotions if these are over-expressed in their social network."[7]

Moreover, not only can over-expressed emotions on social media alter our mood, but they can also alter our values. A recent experiment on the effects of the coronavirus crisis on people's emotions concluded that "based on the dynamic relations of values to each other and the way that emotions relate to values, a negative emotional climate can contribute to societal value change towards values related to security preservation and threat avoidance."[8] This conclusion comes to support what I shared earlier in the book about how the energy we absorb from people and spaces can influence the way we think, feel, and behave, thus preventing us from being energetically authentic.

Energy attack in the digital landscape can be amplified by what's referred to as *filter bubbles* or *echo chambers*. Essentially, popular social media sites such as Facebook and Instagram utilize algorithms that aim to match us up with people and information that resonate with our emotions, beliefs, and values as these are dictated by our behavior on these platforms. Haven't you noticed how after clicking a certain link, engaging with a company's post, or mentioning something regularly in your posts and comments you're bombarded with more and more content on the same topic?

This is the algorithm responding to your behaviors in an effort to keep you engaging in its digital space. The algorithm creates personalized echo chambers that include people and information that resonate with you and your beliefs, and keeps at bay information that disagrees with your viewpoints. Although such groupings can be a good thing when you've taken the time to mindfully choose the people and content you engage with on social media, you can easily go down a negative rabbit hole that creates an echo chamber filled with toxic people, fake news, and attack-filled posts that make you vulnerable to energy attack.

CHAPTER 39

Taking Control of Your Online Presence

N ow that you have an understanding of how the digital landscape works both practically and energetically, it's time to take action toward securing and protecting your online presence. Before we explore various energy and spiritual processes you can use to both clear the energy of and shield your online presence, we first need to talk about the practical actions that you can take to eliminate as much negative energy online as possible. These actions combine measures you can take and boundaries you can place to be in control of the digital spaces and people you interact with online with tactical steps you can take to eliminate negativity when it shows up.

From the Town Square to the Living Room

In 2019 Meta's CEO Mark Zuckerberg published an article in which he shared his view on the future of social media and the internet. In this article he shares:

> *Over the last 15 years, Facebook and Instagram have helped peo-*
> *ple connect with friends, communities, and interests in the digital*

equivalent of a town square. But people increasingly also want to connect privately in the digital equivalent of the living room. As I think about the future of the internet, I believe a privacy-focused communications platform will become even more important than today's open platforms. Privacy gives people the freedom to be themselves and connect more naturally, which is why we build social networks.[9]

In the analogy of the town square and the living room, Zuckerberg not only captures the desire that many of us have for more intimate online interactions, but also the solution for eliminating online energy attacks. In the previous chapter, I distinguished between public, semi-public, and private digital spaces on social media. By making a conscious choice to shift our online interactions away from the public town square and toward the semi-public and private living rooms, we automatically gain more power over the space we're in and the people we interact with.

I personally rarely scroll through the newsfeed on either Facebook or Instagram and instead focus on interacting with people in private Facebook Groups, Messenger, WhatsApp, or Instagram's DMs. As a result, I avoid going down the rabbit hole of endless scrolling and the potential of running into people or information that will upset or affect me in a negative way. Although I pass through the town square on a daily basis when I log into Facebook or Instagram, I immediately go straight to the digital living rooms that I've nurtured with positive vibes and people.

You Are the Mayor of Your Town Square

If you do choose to hang out in the town squares of social media, know that you are the mayor and you get to mold them in a way that amplifies rather depletes your energy. Your newsfeed on most social media platforms includes updates from people you've followed and ads from content you've engaged with. By being conscious of the people you friend or follow, by taking the time to carefully curate a group of people who bring positive energy to your feed, you get to turn your town square into a high-vibe place.

Simultaneously, by being mindful of the content you read, like, comment, and interact with in any way on social media and the internet in general, and by ensuring that you only engage with content that adds something positive to your energy, you let the algorithms know what information to send your way. On occasions when you're fed up with ads and content that you don't want to see, you have the option of letting the social media platform know that you're not interested, thus teaching the algorithm how to serve you best.

Curating a High-Vibe Community

One of the biggest frustrations people face when it comes to curating a high-vibe community of friends and people they follow online is the matter of unfriending or unfollowing people. Due to the increased merging of the physical and digital worlds, our relationships with most people in our lives now exist in this liminal, in-between space. As a result, when the online relationship ends or seems to do so, the physical relationship also suffers. This results in unnecessary misunderstandings, hurt feelings, and drama.

A lot of the spiritual advice given about unfriending and unfollowing people has to do with doing it without reservations or considering the impact it'll have. Although I've supported this view for a long time, I've increasingly realized that the progressive merging of physical and digital spaces has shifted our relationships to the degree that we now need to take a more nuanced approach to managing them. The digital space is no longer a game, novelty, or pastime; it has become an extension of our lives and relationships, and thus our online relationships should be treated in a similar way to our physical ones.

My personal strategy of managing my relationships while also taking into consideration my digital wellbeing includes a combination of setting clear boundaries and taking tactical action to manage my online community. When it comes to Facebook, I've set up two profiles, one for business and one for friends and family, creating a clear boundary between the two and avoiding misunderstandings. Since I only use Instagram for business, I let my friends, family, and other acquaintances know that I only follow people for business-related purposes. As a result of setting clear boundaries on both social media platforms, I get to maintain the connection with my close relationships while also respecting my own wellbeing.

When it comes to unfollowing or unfriending people I'm already connected with on social media, I treat each case differently, realizing that unfollowing or unfriending someone may end up damaging our physical relationship. If this person is a close friend or family member, I'll send a quick message explaining myself, but if it's just an acquaintance, I'll make the change without giving an explanation, as the intimacy of the relationship isn't strong enough to justify the explanation. What's far easier to do than unfriending or unfollowing people is muting those who you don't want to see updates from for any reason. Both Facebook and Instagram have a mute option next to each person's post, allowing you to mute their posts and stories.

Take Control of Your Privacy Settings

Another step to taking control of what you see and whom you interact with on social media is editing your Privacy and Ads settings. Most people don't know that they can actually tell Facebook (and, therefore, Instagram, as it's owned by Facebook) the kind of ads they'd like to see or not see. Exploring the Privacy and Ads sections of the social media platforms you use can help you have more control over the people who can send you friend requests and see your posts, what personal information people can or cannot see, and most importantly, the information you make available for advertisers to use.

I recently revisited the Ads settings of my Facebook account and turned off ads coming from all advertisers, eliminating potential negative or unwelcome ads that could result in energy attack. Due to recent exposure of how advertisers leverage psychographic information on social media to manipulate our behavior, social media companies have become increasingly more transparent, giving us more access to, and control of, our profiles, but also tightening their privacy and security protocols. I want to believe that Mark Zuckerberg's vision will be fulfilled eventually, leading to a future that's safe and secure, and one in which we're in full control of our digital spaces.

Be Intentional

Probably the most important tactical step you can take to protect your energy on social media is to be intentional with it. Social media is designed to be addictive. A great deal of research goes behind the interface of the social media sites we use, which are aimed at keeping us engaging with the platforms for as long as possible. How many times have you logged into a social media site with the intention of doing something specific, only to find yourself sucked into a rabbit hole of endless scrolling and mindless liking for hours, and completely forgetting about your initial intention? In his book *Hooked: How to Build Habit-Forming Products*, Nir Eyal shares that addictive technology leverages our psychology to create external (for example, notifications for new messages) and internal (for example, our need for hope, pleasure, or social acceptance) triggers that get us hooked on their platforms, making them indispensable parts of our lives.[10]

When we pair knowledge about the addictive nature of social media with our commitment to being energetically authentic, we create a strong-enough intention to break out of the addictive loop and start using social media in a healthier way. To do this successfully, take a moment to set your intention and decide on a time limit before you log into any social media platform. What are you going there for? Is it to connect with friends, share something on your feed, or promote your business? Unless you have a clear intention in mind, you'll let yourself and your energy be used by the technology put in place by the platforms' creators.

Turn Off Notifications

The primary external trigger social media and other online platforms and websites use to draw you into their vortex are *push notifications*. Each time a notification pops up on your phone or screen it triggers your internal need for pleasure, creating an almost irrepressible desire to log into the social media platform and check it out. Even if the notification leads you to having a positive experience online, chances are you'll then get sucked into mindless scrolling and potentially stumble onto something toxic or negative.

Turning off all mobile and desktop notifications gives you control over your intentionality of social media. It ensures that you get to be the one deciding when you'll check your phone, as well as the kind of activities you're going to engage in.

Take a Social Media Break

The best thing you can do if you find yourself stuck in a social media energy rut, inundated with toxic people and information each time you log in, is to take a social media break. Taking a week off of social media will help you clear your energy and reset your vibrational frequency so that you cease the negative momentum of attraction you've got going on online. The more energy you give to online negativity, the more it'll continue, so going cold turkey is the easiest way to clear out the negative vibes and start with a clean slate.

Having taken some time off and having raised your vibration, you can then use the tips and processes from this and the following chapter to energetically and physically clear, shield, and protect your social media platforms.

Shift Your Vibration

What ultimately controls your social media experience is your vibration. When you take the time to clear and shield your energy and raise your vibrational frequency before engaging online, you ensure that you only come in contact with people and information that match the frequency you're emitting. No person, social media company, or advertiser can assert something in your experience that you're not a vibrational match to. As you work through the processes in this book and consistently clear your energy and raise your vibration, you'll eventually shift your dominant vibrational frequency to a higher and higher level that naturally protects you from online negativity.

CHAPTER 40

Digital Clearing and Shielding Processes

When you engage in the digital landscape, you mostly utilize the emotional, mental, and astral layers of your aura. When you take the time to clear and shield your aura using the processes discussed in previous chapters, you automatically strengthen your energetic defenses online, too. However, since the digital landscape essentially exists in a separate dimension, you can use additional processes to protect yourself there. In this chapter, I'll share with you three such processes that you can use to both clear and shield your digital self.

Digital Space Clearing Ceremony

Let's revisit the analogy of the digital world being an extension of, and mirror of, the physical world. The various social media sites you use—Facebook, Instagram, Twitter, TikTok, and so on—are akin to digital countries with various cities, neighborhoods, shops, houses, and inhabitants. In the same way you can use various space clearing tools and processes to clear and shield the energy of your house, you can use them to do the same thing in the digital spaces you inhabit.

In a digital space clearing meditation, you access the digital space of your social media sites through visualization and use the various processes you learned in this book, or any other clearing and shielding processes you choose, to perform a space clearing ceremony. By clearing and shielding your digital presence energetically, you intentionally proclaim to yourself and the Universe the kind of interactions you wish to have online. As a result, the Universe responds to your request and orchestrates the right set of circumstances to reorganize your digital spaces in a way that matches your energetic intention. After doing this ceremony, you'll also receive impulses and inspiration as to the practical changes you need to make to actualize these energetic changes.

Follow these steps to perform a digital space clearing ceremony:

1. Close your eyes and get into a meditative state. Take some time to center, ground, and connect to your protection power as instructed in Chapter 8.

2. Visualize yourself hovering over outer space and looking down on what seems to be a digital planet Earth. Instead of the usual continents, countries, and oceans, what you see are the various digital countries that are the social media platforms you use. You can see Facebookville, and Instagramland, followed by Twitterverse and whichever other platform you may use.

3. Choosing one of them, let yourself gradually zoom in and descend into it. Let yourself scroll through the various cities, streets, and neighborhoods of this country. These are the equivalents of your newsfeed, the online groups you're in, your profile, your friends or followers lists, your private messages, and so on.

    As you walk through these digital spaces, notice what you can see, feel, hear, and sense. Use all your senses to scan the place and gauge the quality of the energy there. Maybe some streets and neighborhoods are light and positive, but some turns and corners look dirty and murky. Maybe people are walking around; how do they look and what do they say? Do you enjoy being there? As you explore these digital spaces, make mental notes of what needs to be cleared.

4. Having identified the areas and people that need to be cleared from these digital spaces, use one or more of the clearing processes in Part II to clear the space. You can call upon the fire dragons to burn the toxicity, use an etheric net to clear away the trolls, call upon the sylphs to use their etheric vacuum cleaner to remove etheric stains and cobwebs, or saturate the space with the violet flame to transmute negative energy into pure light.

5. When the space feels cleared of negativity, use one or more of the shielding techniques in Part III to cast an amplifying, repelling, or transmuting shield in the space. Ideally, use a combination of amplifying and repelling or amplifying and transmuting shields to ensure that the energy stays high and that you're also strongly protected and can repel negativity.

6. When you're done with clearing and shielding your chosen digital country, move on to the next one and repeat the process until your digital world feels light and joyful.

7. Before you come out of the meditation, be sure to thank the spirit guides you called upon, asking them to uphold the shields for as long as you want them to.

You can download an expanded audio recording of this meditation at *GeorgeLizos.com/PYL*.

Digital Amulets and Talismans

In the same way you can wear an amulet or talisman to ward off or amplify energy, you can also use them digitally to perform the same tasks in your social media platforms. Since we're working in the digital dimension, these aren't physical amulets and talismans, but digital ones instead.

There are two ways to go about this:

- ⊘ You may choose to share a picture of an amulet or talisman as a post in your chosen social media site. Doing so brings the protective intention of these tokens into the digital dimension, extending their protective powers from the physical to the digital space.

- ⊘ Alternatively, you may choose to turn any other picture, video, or even a written post into an amulet or a talisman. What's important is that you choose an image, video, or piece of text that holds the intention you wish to extend into the digital space. For example, if mountains make you feel strong and powerful, you may choose to share a picture of a mountain that evokes these feelings for you, setting the intention that the mountain acts as an energetic protector warding off negativity. If you have a favorite quote, affirmation, or prayer that makes you feel safe and invincible, you can share that, intending it to repel negativity or amplify the natural auric defenses of your digital space.

There are endless possibilities of what you can use to create your digital amulets and talismans, but the essential component to their effectiveness is the intention you set when you post them. It's important to take a few minutes before you share the post to set your protective intention, instilling it into the post and then seeing it extend its light through your digital space.

Finger Clearing and Shielding

Since your body is your most powerful energy protection tool, you can also use it to clear and shield the digital spaces you hang out in. Finger clearing and shielding involves coming into your power to clear and protect energy, and then mindfully extending that energy and intention to your social media sites through your finger and the technology you use to access them. Similar to performing a digital space clearing ceremony, you leverage the processes you've learned in the book to clear and shield your digital social media countries. Rather than accessing them in a visualization, you instead access them via your devices.

Follow these steps to finger clear and shield your social media presence:

1. Close your eyes and get into a meditative state. Take some time to center, ground, and connect to your protection power, as instructed in Chapter 8.

2. Focusing on your solar plexus chakra, the center of your strength and power, visualize the golden light of your solar plexus growing bigger and stronger with each breath that you take. Let the light expand through your body so that your being is saturated with it.

3. With intention, extend the index finger of your dominant hand toward the screen of your mobile phone, tablet, or desktop, which you have open to the page of your chosen social media site, and visualize the golden light shooting out from your finger and seeping through the screen into the digital space. This golden light is the essence of your strength and power, and it has the ability to both clear and shield your digital spaces. With your mind's eye, visualize this light extending through all the various cities, streets, and neighborhoods of your social media sites, clearing and shielding them.

4. If you want to add additional protective shields, you can choose one of the amplifying, repelling, or transmuting shields and visualize the light extending from your finger into the digital spaces.

5. When you've cleared and shielded all your social media sites, offer gratitude and end the process.

CONCLUSION:
DO THE WORK

There's one last step to energy protection, but before I share it with you, let's take a moment to appreciate what you've accomplished so far. First and foremost, not only have you chosen to take a proactive approach to protecting your energy, but you've followed through with it. Research shows that approximately 62 percent of people who start reading a book don't get to the finish line,[11] but you're not one of them. You've made it to the end. Well done, you! You deserve a pat on the back, so go ahead and give it to yourself.

In our journey together through this book, you've educated yourself on the types of energy attachment that can stain your energy, learned how to identify them, gotten to release them using an array of energy clearing processes, and strengthened your energy field with amplifying, repelling, and transmuting shields. Furthermore, you've extended your newfound skills to the digital spaces you hang out in, and you have created a safe environment for both your physical and digital selves.

Specifically, so far, we've covered six out of the seven steps of the energy protection process: centering, grounding, connecting, identifying, clearing, and shielding. There's one last step we need to discuss and it's by far the most important one because skipping it could jeopardize the entire process. It's called doing the work.

Doing the Work

Here's the truth about all energy healing modalities: they only work to the degree to which *you* are willing to do the work. When you clear and shield your energy, you effect change on your energy body. This energetic shift then transfers through your emotional, mental, and physical bodies, giving you the opportunity to create change in these levels of your being, too.

Simultaneously, your energetic shift sends a signal out into the Universe that proclaims that you're now a different person; this attracts to you people and circumstances that give you another opportunity to make real changes in your life.

The key word in both cases is *opportunity*; you have the choice to take these opportunities and do something with them, or ignore them and stay stuck and stagnant. The former choice is what doing the work is all about.

Let's take a closer look at the two phases of the doing the work process.

The Healing Crisis

A *healing crisis* is a short-term worsening of your state of being before positive change can occur. It can last anywhere between two days and a month, during which you can experience mood swings, unsettling or depressive thoughts, and flu-like symptoms. A healing crisis is a natural outcome of shifting your energy because your mind, emotions, and body also need to align with the shift. Essentially, when you clear your energy, you affect your energy body and aura, which are extensions of, and interconnected with, your mental, emotional, and physical bodies. Although the clearing takes place instantly on an energy level, it takes some time for the change to transfer through the entire system.

The short-term worsening of your state of being occurs because as this process takes place, you may need to purge old thoughts, emotions, beliefs, habits, and toxins that are discordant with your new state of being. At the end of this purging period, and after you've shed energy attachments from all levels of your being, the healing crisis completes and your wellbeing improves.

The pitfall many people fall into during this first stage of the process is that they resist the healing crisis. Thinking that the energy protection process probably didn't work, they suppress the purging of limiting thoughts and emotions, which aggravates them instead. Unfortunately, most of us living in the Western world grew up learning that expressing negative emotions is a sign of weakness, and thus we suppress the process and prevent ourselves from venting and releasing the negativity.

Your challenge through the healing crisis, then, is to be mindful of the limiting thoughts, emotions, beliefs, habits, and toxins that come up and create space for yourself to go through this process. Many additional processes and modalities can help you through a healing crisis. Some of my favorites include journaling, using the Emotional Freedom Technique (also known as tapping) or mirror work, and letting yourself experience a good old crying session.

Different people experience healing crises in different ways and to differing degrees. For some people, it's intense and chaotic, for others it's so mild that it's barely noticeable. As a result, it's best if you don't have any expectations about what you should experience. Instead, be aware of the possibilities and mindful of your day-to-day state of being so that when you're presented with an opportunity to purge, you take it rather than avoid it.

Actualizing the Change

Having done the work of purging energy attachments from all levels of your being, the final step to doing the work involves actualizing your energy work in the real world. Often, we expect too much out of the energy work we do. Yes, energy work is powerful and can help us create massive positive changes in our energy and mindset, but the only way these energy changes can have a real impact is if we get out into the world and actualize them.

Shortly after you're done clearing your energy, and possibly while you're going through a healing crisis, the Universe will bring you real-life opportunities to help you actualize the energetic shifts you've made. You may receive a call from a friend you plan to cut the cord from, you may get inspired to make healthy changes to your diet, you may feel called to make a career change, you may get invited to attend a talk about something, and so on. When these opportunities come your way, it's your responsibility to take action.

It's true; no one enjoys having an uncomfortable conversation to end a friendship, the mess that moving houses brings, or the uncertainty of starting on a new path, but these changes are necessary to complete your energy protection journey. If you only do the energy work but don't follow through with the real-life work, then you sabotage the entire process and keep yourself trapped in a vicious circle of negativity that no process or spirit guide can get you out of.

Remember the mantra I've been repeating through the book: *You* are the one with the power to protect your energy, and this extends beyond the energetic realm to the physical one, too. The toxic people won't go away unless you stop hanging out with them, the negative thought forms will keep finding you unless you get mindful of your thinking process, and the low-level spirits will keep haunting you until you create a positive environment around you.

Although actualizing your energy clearing work in your daily life can be difficult and uncomfortable in the beginning, you'll get better at it the more you do it. In time, and as you embrace the initial discomfort and messiness of change, you'll get hooked to the freedom and transformation it brings, and you'll welcome it rather than avoid it.

How to Move Forward

There are a few options for moving forward from here. If you've chosen to read the book first before applying the processes, it's time to get your journal out, choose your meditation spot, and get started. Download the Protect Your Light Cheat Sheet (*GeorgeLizos.com/PYL*) to keep track of your progress.

If you've been doing the processes and meditations while reading the book, here's your next plan of action:

1. **Revise the types of energy attachments:** Knowledge is power, so the more aware you are of the various energy attachments you

may come into contact with, the better able you'll be to identify and protect yourself from them. It may be a good idea to print the Energy Protection Cheat Sheet and have it on hand to refer to as things come up.

2. **Master your psychic scanning skills:** Effectively scanning for energy attack is essential to properly protecting yourself from it. You can of course clear your energy without first identifying what's there, but chances are you'll miss something. If you're new at psychically scanning energy, spend more time practicing the "Turn On Your 360-Degree Vision" meditation in Chapter 11 to cement your skills.

3. **Decide on your daily energy protection practice:** Your practice needn't be long or complicated. Simply choose the clearing and shielding processes that work best for you and practice them consistently on a daily basis. The more you do this, the better you'll get at it and the quicker you'll be able to clear and shield your energy. I suggest you choose one or two clearing processes that you can use daily to clear multiple types of energy attachments, and only use more advanced processes for special occasions or for intense cases of energy attack. When it comes to shielding, layering an amplifying and a transmuting shield is enough to keep you protected from most energy attack, and then you can use repelling shields as needed.

4. **Keep doing the work:** Remember, your energy protection work doesn't end at the meditation pillow; that's where it begins. Doing the work of creating space for purging your emotions and making real changes that help actualize your energy work should be a daily practice. It'll feel uncomfortable in the beginning, but the more you do it, the more comfortable it'll get, and you'll eventually come to enjoy the freedom and transformation it brings.

5. Last but not least, **take a playful approach to your energy protection practice.** I know that learning about all the ways through

which you can be negatively affected by energy can be upsetting and even scary, but the more you do the work, the more comfortable and safe you'll feel. And, if at any point you let fear get the best of you, come back to the understanding that you're a powerful spiritual being and you have the power to protect yourself. Use the meditation in Chapter 8 to reconnect with your protection power, and once you feel safe and stable, go through the whole energy protection process.

In time, and as you consistently clear your energy and raise your vibration, you'll attract less and less energy attack. You'll create your own positive bubble of attraction that attracts to you people, situations, and circumstances that match the high-vibe person you've become. Then, energy protection will be less about clearing yourself of energy attachments and more about maintaining and further amplifying the glorious world you created for yourself.

NOTES

1 Bessel van der Kolk, *The Body Keeps the Score: Brain, Mind, and Body in the Healing of Trauma* (New York: Penguin Books, 2014).

2 Masaru Emoto, *The Hidden Messages in Water* (New York: Atria Books, 2005).

3 Judy Hall, *Crystals for Energy Protection* (Carlsbad, CA: Hay House, 2020).

4 Yogi Bhajan, *The Aquarian Teacher: International Teacher Training in Kundalini Yoga,* Level 1 (Santa Cruz, NM: KRI Publishing House, 2005).

5 Laurence Hecht, "Mysterium Microcosmicum: The Geometric Basis for the Periodicity of the Elements," *21st Century Science and Technology* (May–June 1988), 18; Robert J. Moon, interview with Carol White (in two parts), *Executive Intelligence Review* 14, no. 43 (October 30, 1987): 31, and *Executive Intelligence Review* 14, no. 44 (November 6, 1987): 18.

6 Katie Brockhurst, *Social Media for a New Age 2, A Digital Self-Care Guide, The Next Phase: 2020 and Beyond* (That Guy's House, 2019), Kindle Edition.

7 Emilio Ferrara and Zeyao Yang, "Measuring Emotional Contagion in Social Media," *PLoS One* 10, no. 11 (November 6, 2015), *https://doi.org/10.1371 /journal.pone.0142390.*

8 Steffen Steinert, "Corona and Value Change: The Role of Social Media and Emotional Contagion," *Ethics and Information Technology* (July 21, 2020): 1–10, *http://doi.org/10.1007/s10676-020-09545-z.*

9 Mark Zuckerberg, "A Privacy-Focused Vision for Social Networking," Facebook post, March 12, 2021, *www.facebook.com.*

10 Nir Eyal, *Hooked: How to Build Habit-Forming Products* (New York: Portfolio Penguin, 2014).

11 Statista, "When Do You Abandon a Book," Statista Research Department, July 9, 2013, *https://www.statista.com/.*

ACKNOWLEDGMENTS

To God Apollo, thank you for inspiring and writing this book through me. It's an honor to follow your guidance and live your path.

To Diana Cooper, thank you for believing in me and writing the most magical and heartfelt foreword to introduce this book to the world.

Thank you, Rebecca Campbell, Emma Mumford, Danielle Paige, Victoria Maxwell, Yasmin Boland, Shannon Kaiser, Gala Darling, Lisa Lister, Dougall Fraser, Sophie Bushford, Amber-Lee Lyons, Amy Leigh Mercree, Cael O'Donnel, and Katie Brockhurst for your generous endorsements and support.

Thank you to the talented Leah Kent for helping me communicate the message of the book through this striking cover!

Thanks to Katie Brockhurst for helping me understand the inner workings of the digital landscape, through our soulful conversations and her book *Social Media for a New Age*.

I'm grateful to Amy Leigh Mercree, my agent Lisa Hagan, my publisher Michael Pye, Maureen Forys, Rebecca Rider, and the entire team at Hampton Roads for trusting in me and this book.

To my friends Val, Sargis, Marianna, Katerina, Emma, and Hannah, thank you for your unending and unconditional support while I was manifesting this book.

To you, the reader, thank you for fiercely protecting your light and channeling it to follow your purpose to create a better world.

ABOUT THE AUTHOR

George Lizos is a spiritual teacher and intuitive healer who is passionate about helping lightworkers to follow their purpose of creating positive change in the world. He's the #1 bestselling author of *Lightworkers Gotta Work* and *Be the Guru*, creator of Intuition Mastery School®, and host of *The Lit Up Lightworker Podcast*.

George has been named one of the top fifty health and wellness influencers by Health Blog Awards, and his work has been featured in *Soul & Spirit*, *Watkin's Mind Body Spirit*, and *Kindred Spirit* magazines. He holds bachelor's and master's degrees in Metaphysical Sciences, a BSc in Human Geography with a focus on sacred geographies, a MSc in Psychology, and he is a priest of Hellenic Polytheism.

Based in Cyprus, George runs a thriving, online international community of empaths, lightworkers, and spiritual leaders within the *Your Spiritual Toolkit* Facebook group. There, he provides daily guidance and holds transformational workshops aimed at overcoming the blocks that keep us stuck and that prevent us from fearlessly following our purpose.

www.georgelizos.com
www.yourspiritualtoolkit.com
Instagram @georgelizos

WORK WITH ME

Get Weekly Tools
Download my FREE *Discover Your Life's Purpose* guide to find and define your life's purpose in a specific, two-paragraph definition. You'll also receive my weekly newsletter with more tools and guidance. Get it at *georgelizos.com/lifepurpose*.

Work with Me
If you've enjoyed this book and want to go deeper, check out my online courses, meditations, and private sessions at *georgelizos.com/work-with-me*.

Get Support
Meet like-minded lightworkers, enjoy guest teacher lectures, and attend exclusive workshops within my private Facebook group, *Your Spiritual Toolkit*.

Feel Inspired
The Lit Up Lightworker Podcast features interviews with leading spiritual teachers. You'll get to fill up your spiritual toolkit with wisdom and guidance to help you follow your purpose and help in the ascension of the planet. Check it out on iTunes, Spotify, Stitcher, and TuneIn.

Stay in Touch
Tell me all about your experience with protecting your light on Instagram (@georgelizos).

Hampton Roads Publishing Company
. . . for the evolving human spirit

Hampton Roads Publishing Company publishes books on a variety of subjects, including spirituality, health, and other related topics.

For a copy of our latest trade catalog, call (978) 465-0504 or visit our distributor's website at *www.redwheelweiser.com*. You can also sign up for our newsletter and special offers by going to *www.redwheelweiser.com/newsletter/*.